The Village Idiot Reviews

PETE SORTWELL

ISBN-13:978-1495933660
ISBN-10:1495933660

DEDICATION

For Lucie.

ACKNOWLEDGEMENTS

I wouldn't be able to get my work into your hands if it wasn't for the help of the team I employ, they work extremely hard to make sure what ends up on your kindle is a high quality. These people are:

Julie Lewthwaite, for her continued sterling work on turning my ramblings into something that I can charge money for.
http://www.mlwritingservices.co.uk/

Graham D. Lock, for the excellent covers he's provided me.
http://www.peopleperhour.com/people/graham-d/animator-graphic-designer-and-illu/177926

I can't recommend these people enough.

INTRODUCTION

I started writing this book after seeing a lot being written about fake reviews on Amazon. Now, to clarify, I don't think a writer or whoever writing great reviews of their own work is a good thing to do. Although having been around the writing 'scene' for a little while I do understand the desperation of writers to get their stuff noticed and the temptation of doing such a thing. Take note I'm not calling myself desperate here. I'm normal. Honest. However, I completely disagree with people panning others' work for no reason other than to help their own sales. It's just plain nasty.

Anyway, there's been enough written about that already and I'm bored of it to be honest. However, it did help form the basis of what this book is. *Shall I wade in?* I thought to myself as I saw Twitter and blogs explode with angry posts. Then I thought I'd do something else. I thought I'd use the inspiration of the situation to write a load of fake reviews myself. Funny ones. Maybe If I posted them the guys out hunting for evil on Amazon would come across them. Maybe I could entertain them a little and remind them that sometimes it's fun to laugh. Or failing that, I could make my mates laugh with them. Then I thought, I'll link them all together and form a story, then I might be able to flog it and pack in work after it sells millions.

Once I'd finished daydreaming I got back to it, got it edited, paid for the excellent cover and here it is.

Some of the reviews in this book have been posted on Amazon all of the products are real. All reviews are four or five stars and clearly marked as being fiction. If any of the sellers or manufacturers of the items would like the reviews removed just give me a shout.

This book is supposed to be light hearted and funny. Nothing serious.

I hope you enjoy it.

Finally, I wrote this book during a pretty sad time in my life, my friend, Dennis Roper passed away on 12.08.12. It has been a pretty good distraction from the sadness his death causes me. Rest in Peace Dennis, I'll miss you.

Pete Sortwell

NEW 3 PANTS PACK MEN'S CLASSIC 100% COTTON Y STYLE BRIEFS TO FIT SIZES SMALL MEDIUM LARGE X-LARGE 2X-LARGE

A sturdy hold, but I think there was something up with the material.

Living alone, I need to keep a substantial number of Y-fronts at any one time. This is due to how far away my mother lives away and not owning a washing machine myself. A couple of these three packs were perfect for my needs.

I must say as I pulled on a fresh pair on the day of delivery, I instantly noticed how supporting they were of little Frank and his two pet bulldogs. They were a very soft feel and made me feel all warm and tingly. Not like some pairs I've owned that made poor Frank feel like he was being kettled during a peaceful protest turned bad.

All was well until I paid a visit to the local funfair. Now, I can't blame the full unpleasantness of the ghost train on the pants, or in fact any of it. They shouldn't allow people to go on alone if they're going to have such scary things in there. I think it was when the carnival fellow jumped out and licked my face that I fouled myself in the most horrendously loose and smelly manner. I feel they should also have stricter control on the food hygiene at these traveling funfairs. The smell that presented itself to my new pants was distinctly similar to the three hotdogs I'd consumed shortly before embarking on the journey of dread (as I've come to call it).

What happened next was even more unfortunate; the rugged fair owner had to close the ride for cleansing and publicly told everyone in attendance it was my fault. Due to having soggy pants, I was unable to flee, as I normally would; this resulted in me being cornered between the bearded woman booth and the hook-a-duck stand. I had to be removed by the police for my own safety.

By the time I'd explained that I wasn't, as the crowd called me, a dirty tramp, I was, in fact, someone who had accidently filled his pants due to the above reasons, some of the recycled hotdogs had started to dry, down the back of the legs mainly but some within the pants also.

As luck would have it I was visiting my mother a few days later and was able to get the pants in a hot wash much faster than I normally manage.

Sadly the pair I was wearing the night of the funfair seemed to have stained, and in some places, glued themselves together. They are, for all intents and purposes, ruined, although I have taken the suggestion from Mother to use the soiled pair to polish my bicycle and a sterling job they are doing, too.

My advice: if you're going to visit the funfair wearing these pants, double bag, don't go on the ghost train, and for God's sake, don't eat the hotdogs. The police might not be so quick to act in your area.

-Brian

T&G WOODWARE FARMYARD CRAZY SIDNEY THE SHEEP TEACOSY

Great cosy, but not so great for wearing.

Being a vicar for a small parish in the south of England, I am expected to hold a fair amount of tea parties and get-togethers for my flock, which is invariably the older ladies of the community. Normally I am gracious enough to allow them to make me a woollen tea cosy. These have been, over the years, of mostly good quality, except the time Ethel Morrison presented one to me she'd managed to fashion together out of her husband's incontinence pads, although we've since agreed not to talk about that. However nice the gifts of knitted tea cosies are, once a year I am visited by the bishop, Desmond. He's a jolly old fellow most of the time, although he has been known to get a little bit on the excited side when around new brides. I think it's something to do with the white dresses. Anyway, last month he was due on his annual visit so I needed something a little more sophisticated. Along with tea parties I also run a youth group for the three local children. Denny, the oldest of the gang, introduced me to the internet and the wide range of everything available. Denny also pointed out this sheep-styled cosy and what with there being sheep kept in the paddock next to the rectory, I decided this was a good choice. I just knew Bishop Desmond would be suitably impressed.

I was amazed at how quick the cosy arrived. We ordered at 3 a.m. one morning and it was with us by 10 a.m. the next day. Denny said he thought it would double as a hat and on inspection I have to say I agreed; it *would* bring a smile to Bishop Desmond's face. Things didn't go quite to plan, though. I'd planned to present myself wearing the tea cosy at dinner, an hour or two after serving the first cup of tea to my guests. I had an Irish coffee myself ... well, several. As I was outside the room preparing myself to surprise Bishop Desmond, Millie Wainwright started to choke on the broiled pheasant I'd spent all the morning, and some of the previous evening preparing. Needless to say, me busting into the room wearing a tea cosy didn't raise the mood half as much as I'd hoped. In fact, it raised the anger of Bishop Desmond, who at the time had just finished carrying out the Heimlich manoeuvre on Millie.

In finishing, I'd say leave the cosy on the teapot and leave the jokes to the younger people of your parish.

Denny seemed to find the whole event most amusing.

-Father Frederick

JESUS FANCY DRESS COSTUME ROBE, WIG & BEARD — ONE SIZE

Superior robes.

The youth group fancy dress party was held last week. Father Frederick only had one rule: the people we dress as must come from the Bible. I didn't buy this item as I couldn't get my hands on Father Frederick's credit card for long enough. I did copy it, though. I used a wig I found in the lost property at the church, one of the altar boy outfits that Father Frederick keeps trying to make me wear at this house, and I nabbed a red piece of felt from the church. (I think they use it to rest the collection plates on.) The sandals I had to steal from one of the other kids, Bobby. I think I pulled off the copy well. Once I'd finished I looked very much like Jesus.

It was a great disguise. And with an added bum bag I was able to nick no end of the vicar's stuff. Getting it into my room at the children's home was easy, too, as they didn't think to look in my robes, they were just happy I'd stopped swearing at them instead of talking to them when I came in. For the first few weeks I'd just wafted past them holding up the Vs instead of talking to them. They're still knobs but at least I can get away with stuff if I don't attract negative attention.

If you can afford this outfit, buy it. If not the picture is fantastic to work from.

-Denny

TENA MEN LEVEL 2 PADS

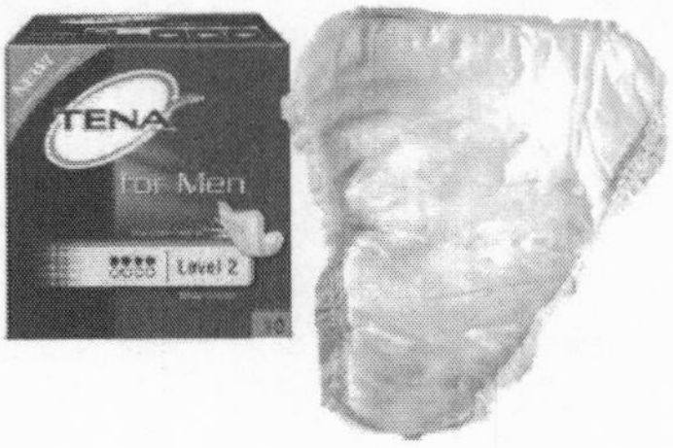

Great! Not just for messing in, either.

Ordering these online is so much cheaper than the NHS charge us. I moved to online ordering after doing a course on computers in the library. It's completely opened the world up for us and saved us enough to go on small holiday to Cornwall.

My husband needs these pads at night time. He does have good and bad days, however, most of the time he is top of his game and we have no need for them. Having these pads around the house (I bought in bulk) got me thinking. One night I needed to keep some plants warm in the garden; tomatoes don't like the frost and I planted them a little early this year. Using a few of these pads underneath the grow bags saved the crop!

It got me thinking about what else I could use them for. So far I've used them for keeping our feet warm when we're outside; it adds an extra layer to our socks and slippers and gave us at least a week extra having tea on the patio this year. I've also used them to cover food when I've made casseroles for friends. I've almost stopped knitting completely due to these pads. They pretty much do everything that the items I normally knit do, Tea cosies, tea towels, you name it these can be used for it. I've made tea cosies for friends too, all have been over the moon with them. My local vicar, Father Frederick, was happy about his, he even told me to keep it secret so as not to upset the people that didn't have one.

To top all the other uses off, these pads are great to be used for what they were designed to do. They hold everything in, no matter how loose or solid.

-Ethel

THE CHURCH GUIDE TO EMPLOYMENT LAW [PAPERBACK]

Informative and educational on British law.

It's always hard being a regional manager. But being a bishop, that's just what I am. It's the same thing. I need to make sure that all my vicars are doing what they need to and keeping the flock of Jesus Christ the Lord in good order. I generally visit once a year. This year I had a problem with one such vicar. He takes care of the smallest parish we have in the south of England. I placed this particular chap in the smallest one for a reason; he's been an alcoholic for as many years as I can remember. A lovely chap, no question, but also a complete and utter liability. I needed to get rid of him, but the law these days just doesn't allow you to send people home and tell them not to bother coming in again the next day like it did when my father was bishop. It's terrible really.

I've given this book a good read and apparently I need to follow all sorts of legal procedure in order to get him gone and even then it'll cost the church money. It seems the only other option, if he agrees, is to put him into rehab and hope for the best while covering his job myself. That's not happening. I can't think of anything worse than hanging about in a small village for up to a year on the off chance he might leave and not drink again. I can't see that happening anyway. He's riddled with the disease.

The final option seems to be taking him off the books, again if he agrees, and retiring him on full pension and housing him for life, while paying someone else to do the job I employed this good-for-nothing for. Something which is equally unappealing.

I think the only option is sitting it out and hoping he either drinks himself to an early grave or stops of his own accord. I'll just hope and pray that he doesn't do anything to bring the name of the church into disrepute during that time. At least if he makes it through to retirement I can get someone else there to keep an eye on him and make sure he doesn't wear his dog collar again. I'll be calling him in for a chat and we'll see where it goes. Maybe there is some sort of damage limitation I can do.

I'm pleased to have the information presented in a nice little book though.

-Bishop Desmond

HEINZ BAKED BEANS 415 G (PACK OF 24)

I love beans and I love charity.

After a pretty disastrous trip to the local funfair, which I won't go into here, I found myself in a pretty ostracised position within the local community. In order to stop the regular parcels of dog dirt being posted through my letter box and smeared over my bicycle, I decided to take drastic action to re-integrate.

I remember seeing someone sat in a bathtub of baked beans to raise money for Comic Relief a few years ago. I like baked beans and I LOVE bath time so decided this would be the perfect way to raise some money for the local youth group. I approached Father Frederick, the local vicar — who was one of the only people I could talk to without being berated for ruining the fair — sharing with him my plans. As the leader of the youth group, Father Frederick jumped at the chance to get some money coming in. He also agreed that it might dissuade others from the dog mess protest that was at its peak around that time. Seriously, someone must have owned a Great Dane or something. So I started the planning.

The event was to take place on my driveway. I had an old tin bath in the shed, all I needed was the beans. I found these and getting them delivered meant not having to go through the ordeal of travelling on the bus. It only comes twice a day and I just needed beans. I bought six crates of beans and also added a few cans of the version that come with hotdog sausages in. I

LOVE hotdogs and thought that searching for the sausages would give me something to do while sitting there; also It meant I could stay there longer as I would have food in with me.

I plastered the village in posters advertising the event, then I went round and re-plastered the village after young Denny went round pulling them all down. The tub was ready, the crowd was gathered, I could even see a couple of girls I like. All I had to do was get into the bath. That was when it all went wrong.

No one told me that when people did it on the TV they didn't microwave the beans to within an inch or their lives before jumping in.

-Brian

DULCOEASE STOOL SOFTENER 30 SOFT GEL CAPSULES

Does what they say on this box, probably without taking the whole box.

I work in a travelling fair, in the food emporium to be exact. I like seeing all the families having a great time and handing all their money over to my family and friends. I used to work on the dodgems but it didn't work out. The boss caught me giving free tokens to some of the local ladies and put me on burger detail. Which isn't too bad, I still get to see the ladies and slip them the odd sausage *big wink* I visited this particular village last year and there was a guy there that was just annoying to look at, you know the kind, they're everywhere. Thankfully they don't get to breed too often, although when they do you get a family of them limping through the fairground, grinning like they don't really understand what is happening. This guy didn't have such luck though; he was so ugly even the ugly girls with learning difficulties stayed away from him. He asked me to make him another hotdog just as I was closing up for the night. There were two ready and waiting for him but the greedy S.O.B wanted three. He wouldn't budge and wouldn't even take the free hamburger I offered him. I'd had a date that night and was ruddy keen to get round there and show her what I'd learned in the bin cupboards around the country after kicking out time. He wouldn't have it, though, and started causing a scene. A scene is never good as someone will end up getting belted then the police are nearly always called and it's bad for business. Being the thoughtful business-minded fellow that I am, I made him his third hotdog, smiled, and carried the resentment of missing out on my date around until this year when I ordered these.

I knew he'd be back. Well, he wasn't going anywhere was he? So come opening night I'd got his three hotdogs ready for him, chocolate flavour or not, he wouldn't notice. The speed he threw them down his neck was like watching a dog eating hot chips.

Terry: 1

Loser at the fair: 0

These work, don't you doubt that. I suspect you don't even need to feed someone a whole packet, either. Highly recommended.

-Terry

STINK BOMBS

Extra smelly, just what I wanted.

My friend dared me to chuck these into the pub. I shouldn't have done it but it was funny to think about all the drinkers in there and imagine their faces once the smell fully became apparent. We bought two boxes. Several got slung into the other kids' bedrooms and once into the staff bedroom before we even got the box out the house. Poor Bobby reacted as badly as anyone could to the smell, he was sick so much he went faint and had to be put in the recovery position for a full half hour. It was so funny when he came round as he thought he was in bed and had been there all night. Watching him reach for the covers that weren't there and tell people to get out of his room set us all off. I think it was the laughter that brought him fully round. When he realised he was actually on the floor of the toilet and not where he thought he'd been, he was up pretty quickly, although he was down again a few seconds later when he started heaving again.

On the night we took them to the pub, we sneaked out after the staff had gone to bed, as we always do. Village pubs always do lock-ins and what with the police only ever being out this way looking for care kids to either return them to the home or demand we stop doing whatever we're doing, it was a safe bet that we'd get away with it. I think they're supposed to have one awake and one in bed, but it never happens. Come 11 o'clock they're all in the staff quarters and we're left to our own devices. Really, we're doing them a favour by going out as they get a better night's sleep without us there. If we couldn't get out, we'd make sure they were kept awake so long they started thinking about leaving and getting a proper job.

There is a special knock to get into the pub out of hours; everyone knows it, even the police, so I'm not sure why they have it. Maybe to feel special, I don't know. We'd caught on to it a long time ago. All you have to do is sit outside for half an hour and listen to how people knock in a strange way. It's easy.

The plan was simple: post the stink bomb through the letter box, bang on the door, and let one of the drunks break them as they came to see why the special knock hadn't been used. Then simply sit back and watch. It took a couple of knocks for the desired affect to kick in and we even had to break the emergency spare bomb we had with us to check how bad they were before we went and knocked on the door again. Then, after no less than three minutes, the door opened and the fun started. It was like a scramble to get out. Old, older, women, glasses — the lot, all got trampled on in the struggle to get out. A few people headed back in once they got close to the door and the epicentre of the smell only to find themselves trapped in a smelly place guarded by an even bigger smelly area. One person came flying through the closed window. Seriously, it couldn't have gone better had it been fire and not a foul smelling glass capsule. We were in the phone box across the road absolutely wetting ourselves. The locals were blaming each other, screaming and shouting. A couple of them even started fighting, only to stop when they rolled too near the front door of the pub and start chucking up over each other.

We had to leave soon after that as the lights around the village green were coming on and people were sticking their heads out to see what all the fuss was about.

These bombs are excellent. I would liken them to the kid-in-care version of a dirty protest. We're definitely going to go out again and do some more bombing. Maybe in the church next time.

-Denny

HIGH VISIBILITY SAFETY VEST

Cheap and loud

I bought this for my mother, she keeps going out in the night and collecting things. Well, actually, she goes out at all time of the day and night and looking for things to collect. I'd like to tell you that she does it because of dementia or something, but she's always done it. Ever since I was little I can remember her hauling an old shopping trolley about, collecting items and bringing them home to pile up in the garden or shed — never to be used again. She always thinks she'll find a use for it but I've never known her to actually use much of it. Except the dead livestock, she always uses that. I grew up on rabbit pie, lamb stew and hedgehog surprise — which isn't as bad as it sounds, by the way. Well, it is, but it's a hedgehog so there is very little meat on it. It tastes a bit like adder, not chicken like most people say other meats taste like, adder. The snake. That was also something she was keen on bringing home.

Recently she's been attacking more and more people. Again, I wish I could tell you it is because of her age but she's always been a feisty old goat. I'm not sure where she got it but somehow she got hold of a police baton and hasn't been shy in swinging it round. I've tried to get it off her but it's something she won't let go. It's her safety net, if you like. It certainly keeps those horrible little sods from the children's home at bay. They mock her all the time. It winds her up and she goes into the dark place in her mind, obsessing about hurting them. That's why I've bought her this; when she's maddened she doesn't or can't see the world around her. What with a spate of drink driving going on and my mother's habit of wandering around in the dark, I thought this would at least go some way to protecting her.

Getting her to wear it was harder than I thought. I'd planned to just leave it outside her house in the hope she'd see it, pick it up and think, 'Oh, free jacket,' before putting it on. She did see it and pick it up, but as far as putting it on went, she wasn't interested. Her plan was to hang it over her really important finds in the garden so she knew, in the dark, what pile they were in.

Oh well, It was cheap as hell. Maybe I'll get more until she's filled her garden and the only thing there is left to do with it is wear it.

-Janet

MONUMENT 147 0F SMOKE PELLETS (PACK OF 10)

Perfect if you live in a care home and/or a boring village.

These are great for scaring the staff in the children's home. A load of us bought some. We started small and set one off down the garden. All you do is pop the top off and sling the bomb wherever you want the smoke to go, and just like Aladdin a puff of smoke appears. Firstly, we chucked it in the bushes at the bottom of the garden while playing football. The staff had the fire engine out and everything. We all had to gather in the car park and try not to laugh too much when then chief fireman came out to report that there was no fire, nor ever was. The social workers all threatened to stop our money, but we've all been around long enough to know that they can't do that even if they wanted to. It's illegal. Good job too, really, as we snuck out our room later the same week and chucked one in the staff sleeping quarters. That went down as well as you imagine. It was funny to see the two staff come out in their pyjamas and night dress coughing and swearing at us. Finally we waited until they were in the office moaning to the home manager about it.

After we'd all been hauled up about it and threatened with more unenforceable things we decided just to synchronise the final attack and get them when they were all in the office patting each other on the back for the rollicking they'd given us not five minutes before. Me and Barry were in the hallway and Ollie and Bobby were in the garden. It only took us sixty seconds from when we left each other in the lounge to when the smoke bombs entered the office from two ends of the room. If it wasn't for the instinct in us to run as fast as we could, laughing all the way, we'd have jammed the door shut, but it wasn't to be and we never got to see them crawling out on their hands and knees.

The police came later that day and did room searches so the few bombs we had left, we lost. The police can enforce punishment and poor old Bobby got a few months' lay down in Juvie. Well, he was the only one whose room I could put the bombs in as everyone else was smart enough to lock theirs.

-Denny

HOPPA 47 LITRE FOLDING LIGHTWEIGHT SHOPPING TROLLEY SHOPPING BAG ON WHEELS

Doesn't explode.

I use this to transport items I find in the street and woods around. I find all sorts, me. There is so much waste in the world I feel it's my place to make use of things. As you know there are people dying in the world. I feel my own brand of recycling is helping those people in some small way. It also gives me more money to spend on sherry, to which I'm fairly partial. Some people in the village call me a tramp or an oddball; they don't say it to my face, of course, they normally drive past shouting it out their car window or daub it over my house. Either way they say it and they're wrong. Just because I get to eat for nothing is no reason to single me out. My dad told me that. He was the one who taught me how to make road kill surprise. Animals getting killed on the road is sad, of course it is, but as long as it isn't the local teenagers from the children's home in a stolen car doing it on purpose again, then we just have to accept that accidents happen. It's nature. And where nature provides, I'm there to take. This cart will carry at least thirty dead rabbits at a time. The wheels are made of quality rubber. They'll go over fields, mud — anything. I've even had most of a sheep that I found near the river in the cart. I say 'most' as I couldn't find the head. Someone must have got there first. I've had other trollies before and they've just not cut the mustard. My last one spontaneously blew up. It must have had a rabbit with mixy in it or something. I had to abandon cart and contents where I stood. I kept the handle though, I'll find a use for it, a spare for this one, maybe?

I can take the bag off and get it in the wash when there is blood to remove from it. It's also got a couple of different pockets on it, too, one I keep the wood I collect in and the other is strictly for Polo mints and my tablets. Polos are the one thing I buy. I've always liked them. If I could live on them alone then I would. They also hide the smell of sherry from my breath when I go to the doctors. I think I like Polo mints even more than I like the tablets the doctor gives me for my nerves. Years I've been on them. I wouldn't stop now, though, too dangerous. I wouldn't be able to not care what people think without them, the doctor agrees and says I'm allowed to stay on them.

Oh, one last thing about the trolley: if you're going to use it to transport dead livestock, don't leave them in it overnight, that's when the flies come. It's not something you want to wake up to.

-Ethel

PANASONIC V700 FULL HD 1920 X 1080P (50P) 3D READY CAMCORDER - BLACK (1MOS SENSOR, 46X INTELLIGENT ZOOM, SD CARD RECORDING, 28MM WIDE ANGLE WITH FACE RECOGNITION) 3.0 INCH LCD

Great zoom function.

There's always something crazy happening round where I live. None of us get out very much. I've only had the internet myself for a year. It's given me such a new lease of life, though.

I bought this in the hope of making a little money to go towards the Thai wife I'm saving up for. I thought I could send in some videos to 'You've Been Framed' or, once I've learned how to, upload them to YouTube and earn some money that way. I've seen others do it, but I've no idea how. All my bride savings have gone on this camera and another book on how to make money from the internet.

I've managed to film one funny thing so far. Brian, one of the guys I went to school with, messed himself on the ghost train at the fair. I didn't get that bit on camera though. *unhappy face* I did, however, get the baying mob cornering poor old Brian and making him cry near the hook-a-duck stand. Him wailing with soggy pants was one of the funniest things I've ever seen. I was so pleased to have this full HD camera with me as I was able to zoom in on his little scrunched up face on my computer and it isn't pixelated at all. I even managed to get my howling laughter out the video, but keep Brian's in. I left the jerky camera movements so it looked more authentic. It's a great clip.

Another thing I saw was the local bag lady having one of her screaming and spitting episodes at someone really early one morning, I caught it all on tape, you can hear me trying to goad her further, but unfortunately I was too far away for her to hear my spak noises. It was another victory for the great zoom on this camera, though. I hope they invent sound zoom soon.

Unfortunately 'You've Been Framed' replied to my submission and told me that they didn't feel this sort of thing was funny. I knew it had gone downhill since Jeremy Beadle left, but I didn't realise it had gone that far. I'm considering contacting ITV and letting them know how far removed from the comedy master that was Beadle they've gone. I suspect the big cheeses don't even know their producers are rejecting this type of gold.

-David

MEN'S NEW MEXICAN PONCHO WILD WEST FANCY DRESS COSTUME

Nice get up but doesn't protect you in a fight.

We always try and have a bit of a party when we've finished the summer season. Working on a fair is great fun for the summer, but once it comes to an end it can leave you feeling low and pretty lonely. For three or four months you get to travel the different towns and villages being Jack the lad, the one all the locals are fascinated by and attracted to, then you become just a man living in a van — which is not what I left school with no qualifications to do. There are 14 travelling fairs in England at any one time; some are linked by family name, some aren't. Everyone knows each other and by and large, gets on. I asked my boss if he thought us all getting together for a bit of an after party was a good idea. His reply was that as long as Mad Michael from Michael and Sons doesn't get invited then he was on board. That was an across the board response. No one likes Mad Michael, mainly because he's mad — and not in a good way.

Almost everyone I invited came. We held it on the green of the last village we were in. We'd loaded up all the stalls and rides beforehand, just to make sure we didn't get any locals wandering over for a quick go on the hook-a-duck. It was for fair folk only. It wasn't a fancy dress affair per se; however, I'd been meaning to get into the Driscoll twins for years now and I knew they'd gone on holiday to Mexico last year so I thought this would be right up their street. I wasn't wrong. When they saw me they couldn't stop smiling and pointing over at me. All

I had to do was wait until their dad and two brothers were occupied elsewhere and make my move.

I'd filled the water pistol up with tequila to add to the Mexican feel of things and once I was sure their family were busy losing all their money to mine in my boss's trailer, I went over and started spraying them. They loved it, opening their mouths and taking all the little pistol could throw at them. It was only when I managed to spray one of the girls' fags that things took a turn for the worse; her whole hand went up.

Things went from bad to worse as instead of putting her hand out she proceeded to start belting me with it and hollering all sorts of names at me. Travelling fair parties are never quiet affairs, but no matter how wild or loud a party could be, nothing could stop everyone seeing an extremely upset twin slapping a man with a burning hand while the other shouted encouragingly.

My sombrero was stolen in the fight, the fake tash I was wearing also caught fire, and to top it off the other twin worked me over good and proper with her high heeled shoes; ribs and kidney mainly, but I took a few to the face and neck, too. I thought it couldn't get any worse, but once the twins' brothers heard about what had happened, they joined in, too. I'd barely made it to my feet when their punches and kicks rained in. It only stopped when they realised no one had put out their sister's hand yet. She must have had a very high pain threshold as she didn't seem too concerned. My boss dragged me into his trailer and locked the door and my ordeal finished, although it very nearly started up again when the brothers realised all that stood between them and me was a thin aluminium door. They gave up in the end though.

The boss told me that part of the deal he'd made to stop me getting buried that night was that I'd need to leave my job. So, limping like a wounded animal, I went in search of somewhere else to live.

-Terry

PETE SORTWELL

FUN SNAPS — 10 PACKS SUPPLIED

These go with a bang (and a splat).

Living in a village is dull. Really dull, I don't get up to much at all. There's a youth club run by the church every week although it's not really fun, and there ain't many youths. The highlight is making Father Frederick do silly things without knowing they are silly. I got him to wear a tea cosy on his head once, that was funny, especially when he did it thinking it would make his boss laugh — and it didn't.

The fair sometimes comes and parks itself on the village green, too. This year though, the local weirdo, Brian, ruined it by making a mess in the ghost train. The whole place stunk and no one wanted to go in it after that.

Emma, the barmaid at the Lamb and Whistle, asked me if I'd help seek revenge Interested, I agreed. All it involved really was ringing Brian's doorbell after lighting a big bag of dog mess on his porch. I bought these, to add a little spark to proceedings.

It couldn't have gone better. The bag was alight, the flames tall, and the crackers where sandwiched between two giant logs. Brian came out, saw the flames and after unsuccessfully calling for help from his neighbours, immediately started stamping like he was doing some kind of ancient African dance. It was when he stamped on the fire crackers that it really went bad for poor old Brian. They started cracking and there must have been a few huddled together in between Emma's Great Dane's dirt as there were a couple of normal short snaps, but then there was a bigger, more furious bang,

26

causing Brian to lose his footing and trip, falling face first onto the grass in front of him. As he fell, the foot that had caught the last lot of bangers had got caught in the brown mess inside and the bag was catapulted, still on fire, into the air. It came down and landed squarely on his back.

There was no shortage of local villagers willing to stamp out the blaze this time. Brian was OK, he didn't need hospital treatment or anything. He did need a good bath and a new pair of slacks, though.

-Denny

GELERT MINI HAMMOCK —
OLIVE/STUFFSACK

Painful but funny.

I've never had a lodger before, never even thought about it, but the other night I was in the Lamb and Whistle when this guy come in battered and bruised needing somewhere to stay. He'd been kicked off the fair that had just finished on the green. Not sure what he'd done, but he'd upset them, that's for sure. All he had with him was his kitbag and a large brown envelope of cash that he'd saved up over the summer. I didn't like the look of him much, nor his accent, but I did take a very keen interest in the cash he had. We got talking and once I'd given him the bad news of how far away the nearest B&B was, how much it cost, and how long ago the last bus had left, I gave him the *piece de la resistance* and told him I had a spare room. I didn't tell him there was no bed in there, or in fact electric, or that the room was actually an outhouse, that didn't seem to matter; it was a place for him to lay his head and that's all he needed. I already had a spare pillow, I found it outside one of the neighbours' houses, It had some weird face drawn on it but I washed it off and put a zip up case on it.

Terry was happy with the room, although he did insist on sleeping on my couch until I got him somewhere to proper to lay his head, that's when I started looking online for the cheapest possible solution.

This is it.

Nailing it to the wall was easy. I made Terry do it.

The only thing is, I wish I'd installed some CCTV in the room as watching him getting in and falling out was one of the funniest things I've ever seen. Somehow the hammock managed to fling him out with more force than he'd put into clambering in. He re-opened some of the cuts on his face on the last try I witnessed, that was a low point (for him). I left him to it then, but looking at the state of him the next day, I'd guess he was in and out of it all night, in fact for the first few nights. We had to watch a video on YouTube in the end explaining how to get in without hurting yourself.

He's a good lad though, is Terry. We've already picked out the person we hate most in the village. Terry does a very good impression too. I think he'll be the perfect housemate. At least he will until his envelope of cash runs out.

-Jock

SECURITY DUMMY SECURITY DOME CCTV CAMERA LED LIGHT

It's OK but would be better if it recorded.

I bought this camera dome for my son, Brian. He's been getting some problems in the village he lives in. It's his own fault for messing himself at the fair and ruining things for everybody. He's always been a scaredy cat. Hopefully this will stop the teenagers smearing dog dirt onto his bike. I can't afford a real camera.

Update: It didn't work, Brian is still having to deal with the dirty protest by locals. I'll have to go back to the drawing board. Also someone smashed the camera. They must have guessed it wasn't real.

-Brian's mum

My mother bought me one of these to stop some of the antisocial problems I was having. I fitted the camera myself, very it easy it was, too and I have to say I felt safer knowing it was up and protecting me. However, after the second night the unit seemed to have developed a fault and blown up as when I went out in the morning it was smashed and the batteries, that I assume were for the flashing light that I hadn't quite worked out how to switch on, were lying on the ground in amongst the broken plastic. I'm returning for a full refund.

-Brian

These look OK. In fact for fake cameras they look pretty close to the real thing. A word of warning if you're thinking of buying and installing one of these, though. Don't Sellotape it to a wooden porch steed with no wires leading to it at all. The locals will guess it's fake.

-Denny

CLASSIC CATAPULT

Bombs away!

Great catapult. Easy to conceal, lightweight, and dead easy to aim. I found it fires AA batteries very well.

-Denny

SELF ADHESIVE FOAM WEATHER STRIP 2 PACK WINDOWS/DOORS

Good excluders but not so good wallpaper.

I became homeless (that still makes me shudder to say) while out in the middle of nowhere. Having a whole summer's wages I could have moved home to Scotland, but seeing as how I'd been chased out of there in the first place I thought here was as good a place as any to settle. The locals seem friendly enough, although no one stopped the kicking I got from a family that I was working with. Mind you, I wouldn't have stopped them, either. If it hadn't been happening to me I would have carried on with my day and thanked my lucky stars I wasn't the guy on the ground wishing he'd pass out. Anyway, once I'd picked myself up and decided alcohol would help, I stumbled into the pub looking for a pint and a bit of good old village sympathy. I had to make do with the tea towel to wipe my blood up and sneering from the barmaid's boyfriend who seemed to be there solely to warn people off talking to his bird.

It was a pretty good night and luckily I managed to talk one of the old soaks into letting me stay at his. He did lie a little about the 'room' he had, which turned out to be a brick outhouse or, as I saw it, a coal shed. However, it did have potential and after a little talk he agreed that if I rented from him I could eventually buy it and turn it into an annexe. He didn't have a bed, though, so I made sure I wasn't going to sleep in there until he did. Unfortunately he heard 'buy a hammock' which was what he presented to me a few days later.

I think he might be a little bit simple.

That brought problems of its own. I won't go into all that, though, as it just brings back the neck (and back) pain. The other problem I quickly encountered was the cold. Those old brick buildings are not good for keeping in the heat. This stuff at least blocked the cracks in the wall and around the coal hatch. In fact I bought a few rolls and plastered every wall with them.

They work well, although I was still a little cold and decided I needed some insulation. Walking home from the pub one night I found a couple of old rolled up carpets. I was far too drunk to get them home that night, but I went back first thing to collect them. It was then I encountered one of the local weirdos. Some old lady had a pair of garden shears and was cutting up the carpet and putting it in her shopping trolley. I cannot even begin to think what she was going to do with it. Unfortunately for her, she was an old lady and so didn't have the strength of someone who used to work the dodgems. She wasn't a very good loser as it happens, either. Screaming like I'd just wrestled her child off her and not a bit of manky old carpet. I'm not sure why, I think it was the crudeness of her swear words that just made me start laughing. I'm sure If I'd read a book on old people or mental people it would have said not to laugh (or point) at them when they are having a paddy. I haven't though so that's what I naturally started doing. It didn't calm her down or make her realise what a fool she was making of herself, though; if anything it enraged her further.

I bet there aren't too many old women that keep police issue batons in their little carts. This one did, though. I'm fairly sure she was prepared to use it, too. If it hadn't been for all the spit and dribble coming out her mouth then I'm sure she would have been able to grip it as she swiped it and thank God for the spit of old mad people as it saved me from what would have been a beating that would only have stopped with the death of one of us, and I reckon her anger would have taken her through to the finish line of that particular race.

Well, you know what they say, an angry cat is an awake cat.

The Volvo parked outside the telephone box wasn't having such good luck as me, though, because the baton went straight through the window. I thought they were supposed to shatter, but it must have been old glass or something as the window smashed as if it were a milk bottle, echoing round the village green and causing the few people that hadn't already come out to watch what was going on to finally get up to tell whoever was causing the racket to shut it.

I scarpered, deciding that she could keep the carpet. I'd think of her paddy the next time I was cold and hope the laughter kept me warm.

I might even buy a bit more of this tape and double up in the outhouse. That'll work too. And if I buy from Amazon I won't have to risk going out, which lowers the chances of the local mad lady spitting in my mouth again.

-Terry

ST JOHN AMBULANCE STATUTORY 10-PERSON FIRST AID KIT

I feel safer with it in the house.

After tripping over on my front step in a dog dirt related accident, I found myself questioning the helpfulness of the local villagers. After slipping over, I found myself face down in my garden at least three hours later, covered in bruises and abrasions. No one had called an ambulance but someone must have seen me as the fair was in town — right outside my house. Not having much in the way of a first aid kit, I had to wipe myself with a stained tea towel. This brought problems of its own — infections, mainly. It also was hard and just caused more pain. After hobbling to bed and trying to make myself feel better with some online entertainment, which didn't work, I ordered this kit. I am now safe in the knowledge that if any more vicious domestic accidents happen, I'm covered.

-Brian

SINGLE KEY FINDER/LOCATOR V3 — NEVER LOSE YOUR KEYS AGAIN

I love not losing my car.

I bought this item not only because I keep losing my keys, but because I've also misplaced my actual car a couple of times now and it's a little embarrassing rushing round the village asking people if they've seen my Volvo. This gadget has been a real Godsend in that department. I can park my car wherever I want and stagger home without having to leave a crumb trail or trying to remember where on earth I was the night before. The receiver is in the windscreen and I simply walk around the village with the airs and graces a vicar should and, holding the button in my pocket, discreetly press it sending the signal bouncing about to find my car. It's got very good range and the noise is audible from twenty paces.

A couple of points I'd like to make is that the sticker that covers the receiver is very small and hard to see. I almost stamped on the unit out of frustration at it not working shortly after I unwrapped it. Luckily I was helped with this by the local tearaway, Denny. His keen eye saw the problem very quickly.

The only time I've had any issue with it whatsoever is when my car was vandalised during the night. Someone threw what seemed to be a police baton through the windscreen. In doing so they knocked the unit under the driver's seat, causing the battery to fall out. Lord only knows what sort of person randomly smashes a Volvo windscreen with a baton. It wasn't the police as I know the local bobby, Bob, and he is not the sort to smash things up willy nilly, other than old man Jones's shed when he was a lad, but he's spent his life apologising for that. It will remain a mystery, thankfully, unlike where my car is parked. And that is all thanks to this litte gadget.

-Father Frederick

BUG ZAPPER

Deuce!

For some reason there has been a large amount of flies, and other insects for that matter, but bluebottles mainly, congregating on my porch of late. It's started to become fairly unsightly, not to mention unhygienic. Even walking over to my bike, which seems to be suffering from the same infestation, can cause huge problems what with all the flies scattering at the sound of me coming. They were getting everywhere and there is only so many times you can get a mouth full of flies and put up with it.

It had got to the point where I was struggling to see the village green through the sheer amount of flies there was. They must have been breeding at some kind of record rate as in the space of a week they'd multiplied to an amount that made me take drastic action.

Searching online I found this little number.

I must say for something that runs on a couple of AA batteries, this thing REALLY BLOWS. What's really great is that the flies pop loudly on impact with the racquet. It gives you a sense of having achieved something.

It became a serious pastime of mine, I even let the local tearaway, Denny, have a go with 'Dangerous Dave', as I've come to call my Bug Zapper. Denny wasn't very good, though, as there'd always be loads left when he'd finished. I properly got into it. I even started to lose a bit of weight. I got a proper tennis outfit so I could put on a bit of a show for the villagers who stopped by to watch me blasting the little swine and I watched videos of Andy Murray on YouTube to get my stance and swing right.

I've managed to get rid of all the live flies now, although I didn't manage it until I banned Denny from 'helping'.

I just need a dustpan and brush now to clear all the bodies, it looks like a war zone outside my front porch.

-Brian

10 X HARIBO TANGFASTICS MINI PACKS

A flying favourite.

Father Frederick buys these silly little packets for the youth club. I much prefer the larger bags. He saves those ones for himself though. He's selfish, that's the only word for it. Brian, the guy who ruined the fair, had a fly problem outside his house after some young tearaway smeared Great Dane droppings over his house and bike. It was funny watching him out with an electric tennis racquet trying to kill them all. For some reason he started wearing tight, white short shorts and a string vest when he was swinging the racquet about. Seeing him making a fool out of himself was such a laugh I didn't think it would be good for the old ladies for it to stop happening, they were laughing their heads off, so when Brian asked me to help, I didn't say no. I had my ultra-small packet of Haribo with me and quickly thought of a solution to the end of the elderly's afternoon of entertainment. I emptied the packet into my mouth in one go, got an immense amount of spit swirling round them and liberally slung the sweets, one by one, around the porch area. They were so sticky they stuck to pretty much whatever they hit and the flies instantly covered them.

We managed to get another week's worth of watching Brian becoming more and more dance-like with his tennis racquet. I had to give up in the end as there were far too many flies for me to want to walk near them with a mouthful of sticky sweets.

I think I've just about paid Brian back for ruining the

funfair.

-Denny

SILVERLINE 675189 700MM BURNING TORCH KIT

A portable incinerator.

This was just the ticket for burning the bodies of a thousand (or more) flies that I'd managed to kill with a bug zapper. Thinking back, this would have probably been good for killing them too, but it didn't come up in the search bar on Amazon when I was looking.

This really puts out some flames and before I knew it I'd burnt all the bodies. Me being me, I got a little carried away with it and lost my doormat in the conflict but that's OK, I rarely wipe my feet anyway.

A great tool!

-Brian

BURGUNDY STA PRESS TROUSERS MOD/INDIE 32-40

Nice slacks — in the 80s.

Having been kicked out of both my home and job in one evening, I've recently found myself short of clothes to wear. I didn't even have anything to wear for an interview up at the Lamb and Whistle pub the other week. I'd forgotten you actually needed to get dressed up for an interview. I suppose that's what you get from working on the fair for ten years. I didn't even have an interview then. Just asked if I could get a job and was asked in return if I was planning on running off with the money. Of course I said no. 'Good, or you'll get this,' my old boss said, waving what appeared to be a rounders bat at me, then he gave me a money pouch and put me on the hook a duck stand. There wasn't a set uniform, either, more a kind of wear what you wake up in set up.

I put the interview off for a couple of days, claiming I had flu. I wished I hadn't later when I realised I couldn't very well swan into the pub and ask for a pint when I'd called in sick to a job I didn't even have yet. Instead I surfed the web and came across this pair of swanky slacks. I've not had smart gear for twenty odd years, since my mother used to buy me it, in fact, before she ran off. But I do remember something my granddad said once: fashion never goes out of style, so I bought the same outfit. These, a burgundy jumper, some slip ons (with tassels) and some bright white socks. They were soon all here thanks to 'next working day delivery'. I paid extra for that as I'm worth life's little luxuries.

I looked good! Well, I thought I did, anyway. Can you believe someone pointed and laughed at me in the street on the way to the interview? I couldn't. I had to aim a scissor kick at them. I missed, but he got the message, I wasn't to be mocked. I did feel a bit like one of the rough and tough policemen I used to watch on TV as a kid. As the kick went up and down, leg fully outstretched, the dazzling white of the socks and the shininess of my shoes was something to be proud of. I started to wonder if I could become a crime fighter. Sadly my daydream didn't last long as the pub is only round the corner from where I live and the raucous laughter as soon as I walked in soon brought me out of the fantasy. It wasn't like I could start throwing about the now infamous scissor kicks either. I wanted to work there. I had to take it. I nipped into the bogs fairly quickly and assessed the situation. I had two choices: go out and face the public, as I'd have to on busy Friday nights when things got heavy; or climb out the toilet window after first scissor-kicking it out with my snazzy shoes.

It was time to be a man, it was time to do something that my TV cop instinct didn't want me to (for the purpose of that thought process I was a 1980s TV cop; well, I had the outfit). My options were limited. I had to go back out there and face the customers and possible future employer and have them tell me how rubbish my outfit looked. I took a deep breath, checked my side parting in the mirror, and headed out for judgement.

I got the job on the condition I wouldn't wear the outfit I had on again. Even the shoes got a full veto by Emma, the pub landlord.

A normal T-shirt and jeans would have done for the interview, which incidentally was what I was wearing when I woke up that morning. I should have stuck with what I knew. I've kept hold of these trousers for the memories they brought back and sometimes I put on the kit again and think back to the time I almost took out a criminal with an excellent scissor kick.

-Terry

BONG 22" LARGE

Makes everything better, except life.

This bong is awesome! I keep it in the woods behind Mary Woodford's house so the social workers can't find it in my room. They're pretty stupid, but not stupid enough to miss something this big when they do the weekly room ransacks.

I've got a smaller one for home use, not to mention the many, many pipes I've either bought or made in the last few years. If you, like me, live in a children's home then delivery might be a problem for you. Me? I just waited outside every day for the postman, well round the corner, I couldn't wait right outside the home as I should have been at school. The workers would have seen me when they were outside smoking their fags. I almost got caught as the postman pulled up in his van due to the size of the package. Although once I had the parcel, it didn't matter if the workers saw me or not. All I had to do was run and their fat asses wouldn't be able to catch me. Law requires they report me missing if I don't make it to school, however living in the rural section of the county, the police only have to drive ten miles, find me, then drive me to school themselves before repeating the process in the afternoon, so largely they don't bother.

If you like a huge hit in one go, these are the bongs for you. I like nothing better than spending my days in the woods or round my dealer's house sucking on this thing. It makes everything in life better. I can handle the idiot social workers when I've had a few of these. I can be confident around my dealer's daughter, who I like. It's just a win-win for everyone involved. I might buy another one for my mum, she loves to smoke as much as me and the way I see it, it's never done her no harm, so why should I do what the social workers say and stop? It's just another rule they like to enforce. I doubt they have any control in their own house so they come to mine and try to make me do what they want to do. Well, it won't work. I just wish they had a greenhouse in the garden so I didn't have to give all my money to Terry. I'd grow my own then. Maybe I can get the idiot vicar to let me grow some 'tomatoes' in his ...

Now there's a thought.

-Denny

7 DAY SHOP BINOCULARS — COMPACT 10X25 DCF (BLACK & SILVER) — TOP QUALITY GLASS OPTICS

My favourite 'peepers'.

'Keen bird watcher', that's what the locals call me. The truth is, I'm not that keen at all on watching birds, but people thinking I am gives me a great excuse to wander round the village pretending to be spying on bluetits. Oh, I'm looking at tits alright, but not the feathered variety, *wink wink*.

I've a secret obsession with Mary Woodford. We spent some lovely times together as teenagers. Then she broke my heart by dumping me and getting engaged to a potman at the Lamb and Whistle, Mickey Branson. It hurt so much I decided to become a vicar. Mickey dropped her within a year, leaving both myself and Mary to await destiny bringing us together again. She wants me. I know it. And one day she will, too. All the sideways glances she gives me are just confusion. She wanted me once, she's shown she has the ability to love me and she will be mine again.

Along with the respect of the locals that comes with being a vicar, so does the ability to move under the radar, making it easier to indulge in my hobby of watching Mary as much as possible.

These compact binoculars are perfect for keeping in your pockets and when hung around my neck they can be easily hidden by pushing them in between a couple of buttons of my tunic.

The rubberised handles are a Godsend as when up the oak

tree opposite her house, I've been known to drop more than one pair of 'peepers'. It's a bit of a giveaway, broken binoculars in the street, under a tree. Well, if it happens more than once, anyway.

I'm not funny or anything. I just struggle to get the woman I love out of my head, that's all. Everybody loves somebody.

-Father Frederick

PROTEC PROLOC 26" AUTOLOCK AND ASP BATON HOLDER

Better protection than spit alone.

Every woman needs a bit of protection. Moreso if you have a useless, incontinent husband. Country life is OK most of the time, but the kids get bored and then people like me become their entertainment, if we let it happen. This little beauty lets them know in no uncertain terms that I'm not anyone's entertainment. Just to make them that little bit more scared, I told them that the police had given me this to hand out beatings as and when I saw fit to help them keep things in good order. I've used it a couple of times now and just swinging it is enough. People usually think twice about name calling once they see this swinging about in front of their eyes.

It allows me to go about my day, collecting things in peace. Which, if you think about it, is the police's job anyway.

-Ethel

JACK PYKE GHILLIE SUIT

Warm but scary for people when you're not in the woods.

I use this for when I'm looking at Mary's house from the back. It's perfect for moving about amongst the reeds and undergrowth. Night is the best time to be round there as staying still is not something I'm brilliant at and however well-disguised I am it's hard not to make out a human shape moving in the trees. I'm not strange, you must understand that. I'm protecting her. You never know who is out there and this village has a higher concentration of weirdos than anywhere I've ever known.

My advice is you're going to use this ghillie suit in the same fashion as me is; don't stay out all night if you're drinking. I was in the trees one night and had a bottle of brandy that Bishop Desmond brought me for my birthday, I took it with me only expecting to have my usual evening snifter. The next thing I knew it was getting light. I'd somehow lost the bag I carry my suit about in and had to try and make it home wearing this suit. Which wasn't an ideal situation, as you can imagine.

The scream of the Sunday Papergirl could be heard the Village over when I stepped form the trees out onto Cooks Lane, which leads down to my vicarage. Her parents were OK when I popped round later and explained that I'd been bat watching all night but it was a close call.

-Father Frederick

PLASTIC MARACAS (PAIR) — ASSORTED COLOURS

Be like Bez. Buy these!

I saw a notice in the Lamb and Whistle for people to Join Jock Curger's band. Now, I've never played in a band before, but I do enjoy a bit of singing and dancing when Glee comes on the Tele. I've even got a few outfits I put on now and again. I check the Radio Times to see what theme this week's show will be and then make what I can out of the items I have.

Happy Mondays are one of my favourite performers. Ever. Not so much the music, but the one that dances around with his maracas, he really inspires me. I never got to see them the first time round and also missed out on the few reunion tours they did. I did write to Bez once and told him how much I thought of him, but the only reply I got was from the address I sent it to with 'return to sender' written on it. I tried again, then again, then realised I was sending to an address that was the fan club address in late 1989. I was a little disappointed but it was OK because I found these. They made me feel closer to Bez somehow.

The night of the gig came round and I put on my best Bez outfit. Tighter than tight jeans, a T-shirt with Mr Happy on and my old PE plimsolls, put these cracking maracas into the 'bag for life' I'd been saving especially for the night and headed across the green to the pub. Dodging the sneers of Emma's boyfriend I headed to the back room without buying a drink. I figured if I was here for band practise I wouldn't have to. Jock was sitting at the back of the smoke-filled room playing with the strings of his guitar. Without looking up he just screamed some swear words at me that all ended in 'off'.

I wasn't giving up that easily though, so I braved the glare of Emma's partner and sat in the bar having a drink; well, two. I always drink two different drinks at the same time. I think it adds a little something to the drinking experience. This particular night I had a Babycham and a bottle of something blue that tasted like some kind of fruit, although I've never seen a blue fruit, except a blueberry, of course, but that isn't really blue if you look at it closely. Necking the Babycham, I then sipped the bottle. It's a nice way to drink.

I saw a few people roll up and enter the back room; all but one of them came straight back out looking shocked. I hoped that Jock had said the same to them as he had to me, that way he wouldn't have singled me out for the torrent of abuse I'd gotten. Finally someone pulled up on a motor bike and carried in the biggest guitar I've ever seen in my life. I hadn't seen him before, but I'm pretty sure I'd seen his bike speeding through the village, I'd certainly not heard many bikes that loud before. He wasn't sworn at either and stayed in the room, I waited until I heard the noise of the band, necked six Jack Daniel's and a Bailey's and took the maracas from the bag.

I didn't know the tune but just closed my eyes and started to dance as if I was in my front room and no one was there. I went wild. I was throwing in my best air guitar moves it didn't matter that I had maracas and not a guitar, I'd seen my moves in the mirror and was confident I would impress Jock and the others. It must have been at least thirty or forty seconds before the music stopped. I didn't though. I kept going to show them that I could keep the beat just in case the sound system ever went down, it must have been another ten or fifteen seconds before I felt myself being lifted and carried at speed, Jock and the big man had got me under an arm each and were charging me at the double doors. I'd opened my eyes by this point.

It's funny but when bad things happen the human body can put itself into a state of denial even the hardest drug addict would be proud of. My brain told me right up until I hit the gravel that it was some kind victory celebration. I'm not sure they even heard me ask, 'What about a triangle?' as they turned and walked back inside.

In closing, I'd say these are great items, a flashy green colour, good beans inside and lightweight, it's pretty much everything you could ask for in a pair of maracas. I'd probably not try and introduce them to a hard biker-style heavy metal band if I were you, though. It's become apparent to me that it's just not the vibe they are looking for. The maracas are pretty durable though. Only one of them broke when we hit the ground.

I'm just glad it was this item that upset them rather than my excellent dance moves.

I lost my bag for life too. That's 10p I'll never see again.

-Brian

*EASYFIT TEAK WOOD EFFECT VENETIAN BLIND * AVAILABLE IN WIDTHS 45 CM TO 210 CM * ALSO AVAILABLE IN DARK OAK, BLACK AND NATURAL COLOURS* 45 X STANDARD*

They keep the stalkers out.

I needed to buy a decent set of blinds as I have a problem with being stalked. A man I dated over twenty years ago seems to think that one day I'll get back with him. He must be mad, what woman on earth would get back with someone who sits in the trees opposite their house watching them with a pair of binoculars while wrapped in a weird ghillie suit? It's like he thinks I don't know he's out there. But even on the morning he turned up offering me dead rabbits for a pie, I knew he'd been out there all night. I live in a village and have done all my life, I know everyone. There is no danger here, but he absolutely insists he is protecting me. I wouldn't be surprised if I woke up dead one day.

At least with this set of cracking blinds he doesn't get to see me get ready for bed or dance anymore.

We have to be grateful for small mercies, Frederick taught me that all those years ago.

The worst part is if he stopped drinking he wouldn't need to sit outside my house, I'd invite him in. He just doesn't want to do that. I know why people are called strangers now.

-Mary Woodford

PANTHER ROCKETS (2 ROCKETS) ## *(GARDEN OUTDOOR FIREWORKS)*

Wooosh — BANG!

I don't think I'm a pyromaniac or anything. I do like seeing things go BANG. And things that expel a smell or smoke. These things are right up my street. The delivery is high, granted, however, if you've got an idiot vicar that leaves his Amazon account open and a postman that doesn't care who he gives mail too, then these are a must buy.

I wasn't sure what I was going to do with these when I ordered them, I just knew I wanted them. They are as huge as they look, too. The day they came I couldn't wait. I collected Bobby from the bus stop. I hadn't bothered to go to school that day, as I rarely do. We headed back down to the vicarage and went in search of something to fire it at. There is a paddock at the back and there were sheep in there. That was the target. I figured that morally that was OK as I saw on YouTube there are places you can go to in Thailand and fire a bazooka at a cow. This was just our village version of it. We wandered into the paddock but it was too close for comfort, we needed a different firing zone. Positioning ourselves across the road we tried to aim, although that was easier said than done as neither me or Bobby wanted to hold the rocket while the other one lit it. I realised we needed a launcher so I ran back over to the vicarage and ripped a piece of Father Frederick's drainpipe off. The rocket slotted in perfectly.

It launched fantastically well, making a satisfying whooshing sound as it left. Watching it sail through the sky was mesmerising. I almost forgot we were about to blow up a sheep. What I wasn't planning on was for Father Frederick to come haring round the corner at the bottom of the hill just as the rocket was passing the road. The rocket was still going like the clappers. I've never seen an actual rocket launch but this must have been like it. It flew across his path just as he turned into his drive, narrowly missing him. The force from his square Volvo took the rocket off the course we'd sent it on. I couldn't see his face but he started to lose control and floored the car into the drive and straight through the fence, then started going across the paddock. That was when me and Bobby legged it.

The second rocket got launched at the old spitting lady in the village; she's a lot of fun but if she catches you pulling spastic faces at her and going 'derrr' she does spit in your face/mouth then swings at you with whatever she has to hand, normally a police issue baton. She tells us in more lucid moments that they gave it to her to protect the streets, but it's more likely that she either nicked it for found it. No copper in his right mind would give her a bat. She'd collared Bobby a few days before and given him the 'dirty shower' as we all call it. He was angry and now we had our rocket to scare the absolute crap out of her with, it was payback time! We plotted up in the alley next to the old Co-op and waited for her, we'd seen her heading off across the fields an hour before so we knew she'd be back. There was only one way she could come unless she wanted to get wet. And besides which she'd not long taken to walking round in a bright yellow high visibility jacket.

She took her sweet time in dragging her cart up the road. I'd instructed Bobby that he needed to aim high so it went off just over her head, we didn't want a real Thai-cow situation. He's pretty much an idiot though and let his end of the drainpipe drop just as the rocket went through. Instead of legging it the other way we both just stood there gawping at what seemed to be the end of our childhood as we knew it.

The rocket soared just as the first one had, sadly though there wasn't a drunk vicar driving a Volvo to put it off course and it continued towards her. Just before it hit her in the back of the head, it suddenly dipped, the thrust must have gone and it ploughed into her beloved shopping cart instead. I was just about to breathe a sigh of relief, but the opportunity was short lived as the rocket exploded on impact, taking whatever slosh she had in there and most of the fabric of the actual cart with it.

I remembered my motto around about then: 'Run, just run'. So I did. Bobby ran too, although I wasn't waiting about for him to slow me down with his cries of, 'Wait, no wait.' The general children's home motto also kicked in: 'Every kid for himself'. All I needed to know was that he was behind me and in being in that position he was more likely to take the dirty shower or the beating which was a buffer between me getting it.

These rockets are awesome, just don't take your divvy mate with you when you go to shoot sheep or old ladies, that's all I'm saying.

-Denny

RUFUS ROO: THE BIG POCKET TRAVEL JACKET IN BLACK BLACK ZIP — LARGE SIZE (STEALTH)

Substantial pockets.

Village life is simple. We don't need all the swanky stuff that the city dwellers feel the need for. We don't need Bistros or posh and exotic restaurants, nor do we need thirty different types of wine with our meals. We lead basic, but fulfilling lives. I decided to collect the love of my life some rabbits so she could bake up one of her special pies. She probably wouldn't give me any, but then that's just her sense of humour. I set the traps late one evening, then went back early morning. I spent the time in-between just sitting near Mary's house enjoying the night sky and sipping from my hip flask.

The pockets on this waistcoat were absolutely perfect for carrying the carcases back to her house.   I couldn't have chosen a better one. Five stars!

The miserable so and so started screaming and shouting when I turned up with the rabbits for her. You'd think a country dweller would be happy with gifts of game weather it was 5 a.m. on a Sunday or not. I left them on her gatepost for her, should she change her mind.

-Father Frederick

XPLICIT FUNNY 'BANANA' NOVELTY BOXER SHORTS

They bend your banana be aware!

I got these for myself. If I ever get a date I'm going to wear them. I'm still trying to work up the nerve to ask out the girl that I like but I will. One day.

I've got my eye on a couple, actually. Janet, who works in the Co-op, and Emma, who works in the local pub. Neither of them knows I like them yet, though. I'm not sure how I'm going to go about asking. I promised myself I would and now I've invested in these pants it will motivate me to do it.

I've tried them on and they are a pretty snug fit! *massive wink* This must mean I bought the right ones and won't be had up for false advertising once the magical day comes.

My only gripe would be that they are a bit too snug. If I wore them for long Little Frank would end up looking like a banana and God knows what would happen to his two pet bulldogs.

-Brian

MARIGOLD INDUSTRIAL GAUNTLET GLOVES. EXTRA LARGE. HEAVY WEIGHT INDUSTRIAL GLOVE RUBBER LATEX GLOVE FROM MARKET LEADERS MARIGOLD. CLEANING ACCESSORIES POWERED BY THE CHEMICAL HUT.

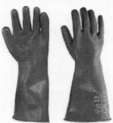

Good for clearing guts up.

Some sick S.O.B stuck a load of dead rabbits in the trees just down my driveway. It took me ages to work out where the rotting flesh smell was coming from. The decomposition was so bad that normal rubber gloves would not have cut the mustard in taking them down from the trees. It wasn't a nice job at all. I'm not even sure if the rabbits were dead before they were strung up.

The gloves did the job as well as can be expected and were able to handle the good hosing down they got once the grisly task was over. I can't fault them in any way.

I've had to buy a pressure washer to clear the area under the trees. There were vermin and maggots everywhere. Luckily Denny, a local kid, helped with the washing. He's a bit of a rascal and needless to say I needed to go in and dry off shortly after handing him the pressure washer. He earned a nice bit of rabbit pie for his work, though.

I was going to pay him, but when I checked my purse I didn't have the £20 I thought I had. He was happy to take a cheque, though.

Hopefully I won't have to use the gloves again. I'm pretty sure I know who left the rabbits and I'll be collaring him shortly.

-Mary

XQ MAX SPORTSNET TENNIS BADMINTON SET — BLACK/RED/WHITE

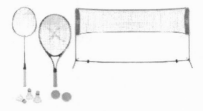

Good but the shuttles have a mind of their own.

Having gotten into the idea of tennis through using my Bug Zapper on a recent infestation problem, I brought this set. I loved swatting all those flies so much, I even lost a bit of weight doing it. Once I'd done the job I started to miss the tennis side of it and thought about trying to get the flies back, although the letter from the Environmental Health department put paid to that Idea. So I hit my favourite online store, Amazon, and found this little beaut.

Unfortunately I almost instantly hit the shuttlecocks on the roof, miles out the reach of me on tip toes with a badminton racquet. In fact, one of the racquets is now also stuck on my roof. So I moved onto tennis. Most of the time the net is up against the wall, unless young Denny comes round then we get a bit of a game going, Denny even brought his own racquet. It doesn't help him, though, he is a terrible shot. The ball goes anywhere but where it should. I had to stop him playing the day one of his poor shots caught me in the throat. I thought my time had come until my breathing started again just before I collapsed.

I didn't manage to play again for the rest of summer, but the kit is safely in my shed and I'm already thinking about using it next summer. Although I won't be asking Denny to play again, he is useless to the point of being dangerous.

It's 4 stars as I lost the shuttlecocks on the roof, and that clearly wasn't my fault.

-Brian

KARCHER K2.300 T50 AIR-COOLED PRESSURE WASHER

Watch the soap, it hurts your eyes.

Old Mary Woodford asked if I'd hose down a minging pair of gloves she'd used to clear away some dead animal or other, and also the ground just off her driveway. I was blown away by the amount of power in this thing — almost literally. I really didn't expect it to be strong enough to cause Mary to scream so loudly when I accidently sprayed her with it. After that I was glad I hadn't put my hand underneath, as that's what I'd thought about doing. I didn't use the patio attachment for the patio. Mary didn't want that doing. I did put it on and just spray mid-air though. It looked pretty awesome, spinning around it created a big soapy cloud, although some of the soapy water caught in the wind and went in my eyes. That stung. I didn't scream, though, I'm far too hard for that.

Mary sent me to clean a couple of cars and the path up the high street after Ethel threw her shopping trolley and the contents about, it was some kind of dead animals. I'm not sure what it is about this village and dead animals everywhere. They could be a cult.

She's invited me back to do some more washing, and I'll do it. Apart from feeding me and giving me a cheque for £20 she is also very lax at keeping her eye on her handbag. £40 for washing a bit of dirt and getting soap in my eyes seems like a good deal to me.

This is an excellent piece of kit, the trouble I can cause with it is endless. It's just a shame you have to have it plugged into

the wall. It's lost a star for not being portable.
   4*

-Denny

SLAZENGER SMASH JUNIOR TENNIS RACKET

Hits stones like nothing else.

This racquet is absolutely brilliant. A guy from the village I live in bought a cheap set and the racquets that came with his were rubbish. There was no give in the strings so it was hard to fire a good shot off. This on the other hand sends the ball flying in exactly the direction you choose. I don't really like the guy I play with, so my main aim of the game was to hit as many of his shuttlecocks as I could onto his roof. I managed to get a nice amount of them up there, and amazingly one of his racquets made its way there, too. He tried to reach up and retrieve one of his shuttlecocks and the racquet got stuck. It was brilliant.

That wasn't the best thing about my tennis game with Brian, though. The best part of the game, and maybe even my life, was when I overhead smashed a fast paced return and it caught Brian square in the throat off the bounce. Before going down Brian started grabbing at thin air in a vain attempt to find something to cling onto. I couldn't stand up I was laughing so much.

It's a shame his mum was so tight that the CCTV (which broke) was only a dummy camera as I would literally give all my pocket money, and 50% of the money I steal from Father Frederick to see that again. The slo-mo shot of that would be completely epic. I would have been guaranteed two hundred and fifty quid from 'You've Been Framed' with that one. We called it a day after that.

The other thing this racquet is really good for is hitting stones across the village green. From outside the pub I was able to hit Brian's front door in quick succession twice causing him to fully believe someone was knocking on his door. The third well-hit stone caught Brian just to the right of his frank and beans area. Again he was down within seconds, although he didn't wait for the fourth stone to hit and dragged himself back inside as if he was crawling through the undergrowth in Vietnam.

A MASSIVE five stars on this.

Buy it, you won't go wrong.

P.S: Don't tell anyone, but it also makes an excellent air guitar.

-Denny

GIANT HIP FLASK 1.9L

Will last the day.

Bishop Desmond called me into the cathedral for a little chat. He seems to think I have a drink problem, or as he put it, I 'indulge a little too often'. Just because I let one of the younger flock talk me into wearing a tea cosy for a joke doesn't mean I'm an alcoholic. He just has a bee in his bonnet and is doing the 'boss' thing because he had to. He was smiling, so I know that's what it was rather than him being serious. He just needed to be seen to be being serious.

He gave me his old hip flask to 'help measure' the amount I'm drinking to a proper 'level'. Which was nice of him. The brandy that was in it made for a nice drink as I was driving home too.

The only problem with his flask was that it was too small and I kept running out. The congregation don't really like the vicar leaving the church halfway through the service to run home and fill up his hip flask. Luckily the day that happened there was an extra-long hymn and I was back just in time. I'd spilt some of the brandy down my dark red robes, although I think I managed to hide it during my closing speech. It had stained the cloth just by my heart and I gave everybody some old flannel about how God loves us all and covered it with my hand while putting on my best loving grin.

Once I got home it was time to seek a solution to the small flask problem. I had a few come and go before I hit the jackpot with this bad boy. Some leaked, some held less than they looked like they would and some just didn't look anything like the one that Bishop Desmond gave me. That was a must, he could still drop in on me at any time and I needed to have something that looked at least a little bit the same, and this fits the bill perfectly. I can get almost two full bottles of brandy in it; the remainder of the bottle goes down nicely with my breakfast time gin and tonic. Once full, I can get to at least supper on this bad boy. I don't always remember finishing it, but come next morning it is always time to refill, and refill I do with the keen enthusiasm that I once held for the church.

I've got a waistcoat with pockets that this fits in easily, so when I'm not wearing my dog collar I wear that pretty much all the time.

I'm thinking about buying another for when I have to go on the annual seaside trip to Skegness with the regional elderly. That's the only time I really need to drink. Being sat next to Bishop Desmond and the vicars from other areas is a right nightmare.

If your normal flask needs filling too often for you, this is the one you've been dreaming about. If you have fear of being called an alky, don't. They wouldn't make these if they thought it would cause alcoholism, would they? No.

5 stars.

-Father Frederick

5 STAR FLIPCHART EASEL WITH W670 X H990MM BOARD W700 X D82 X H1900MM — BLACK TRIM

Attracts idiots.

Since I stopped trucking, I've gotten a little lonely and if I'm honest, bored with hum-drum village life. I go out on my motorbike at weekends, but most of the guys are a little younger and not even near retirement, so they're not around in the week and there's only so much polishing of a bike a man can do (not a euphemism). I've listened to the radio almost non-stop for forty years and I love rock music. So I thought I'd get into something music related. I bought this board as Emma in the pub said I could use the back room for setting up a band. I advertised a couple of weeks before so I could get a couple of weekends' worth of eyeballs on the sign. I just propped it up in the doorway to the back room. The first weekend someone drew a massive knob on the poster I'd spent ages drawing, so I sat watch the second. People are so disrespectful. No one dared do it while I was there.

Come trial night I was eager to see who wanted to be involved. After an hour I did start to lose hope when I'd only had two in, one was rubbish and the other just sat talking to me about guitar strings. The village idiot came in carrying a pair of bright green maracas. He was told in no uncertain terms to get out before he had fully passed through the doorway. After a couple more disappointments we finally had three people. The other guys were much better than me. We were really rocking out. Unfortunately we had to stop when we realised the aforementioned idiot was dancing down the far end of the room, he was going nuts. It was like watching someone on fire trying to put themselves out with their own hands.

After we'd slung him out for good and all we got back to it. The band now stands at three. We're all one person short of getting full numbers.

I definitely have this board to thank for drawing in what is now know as 'Hard Cycle'. We'll be touring soon, come see us.

-Jock

SECRETS OF THE A GAME: HOW TO MEET AND ATTRACT WOMEN ANYWHERE, ANYPLACE, ANYTIME [PAPERBACK]

Like a drug but a book — and legal!

I had an attraction to two local woman and being a bit of a loner who completely embarrassed himself at the village fair (a rather unpleasant experience on the ghost train) I needed a bit of help in trapping these woman into talking to me. This book seemed to fit my needs.

Being a nervous fellow anyway, I took the book with me to where one of the girls I like, Emma, works (the pub), just in case I needed some pointers for any curveballs she might have thrown up. I did as the book suggested and approached her looking confident and asked for a drink. She sneered — not what I hoped for. I kept smiling and looking confident though.

'What you staring at, ploppy pants?' asked her boyfriend at the other end of the bar, causing me to leave without so much as taking a sip of my drinks. So it didn't work out. However I took the suggestion of keeping my options open and headed straight to the Co-op and asked Janet. I must have been out of breath from the march up the High Street I'd just done as her reply of, 'Have you been chased?' threw me a little and there wasn't a toilet in sight for me to go in and consult this masterpiece. 'Haha, no. I'm just keen,' I said adding a smile at the end just as I had read to do. I'm not sure Janet believed me, but no one was more surprised than me when she sighed and said yes! I finally have a date and it's all thanks to the wonders that were provided to me by this book. I have nothing but gratitude for the writers. It completely worked for me.

I am eagerly awaiting the next in the series on how to actually get the woman to sleep with me. I hope it doesn't involve too much showering or girly shaving.

-Brian

EASY2GROW 2 POT HYDROPONIC STARTER KIT

High grade 'ponics.

I thought I'd start small on my growing business and this kit looked like it would do the trick. To be honest this was the only one I looked at. I couldn't do much searching because Father Frederick was only away from his computer for a while. Once it came I was able to germinate the seeds I'd got from a different website and followed the instructions I found online to get my crop planted and well on its way.

So far I've managed to tend to the plants well. The buds are growing and I've tested them using the bong I keep in the woods. All is well.

I don't have a problem with the item, more some advice for anyone who may be in care, like me, and cannot tend to their crop every day. What I've done is buy a timer switch for the lighting and allowed that to work its magic. I haven't worked out a solution for the watering yet, however I have found that if I leave the plant in a dish with water underneath and give it a good watering, covering the leaves and pot before I go then I can get away with visiting once every thirty hours or so. I've got two pots on the go and am having to keep the crop fairly small. This was a test kit really and once I've smoked what it produces the first time I'll be saving for a bigger lamp and better kit to set up in my business properly. My mum even said she'd give me some money for my fifteenth birthday towards a proper set up. It's nice to be able to do something that makes her feel proud enough to offer some money.

This is the perfect starter kit for anyone who is interested in growing exotic plants indoors.

As long as you remember it is all about location, location, location. You don't want to get caught, pick an idiot's house. DO NOT TRY AND GROW THIS IN YOUR CHILDREN'S HOME. It just won't work, the other kids will grass you up before any of the social workers smell it.

Keep growin'!

-Denny

XBOX 360 CONSOLE

Not as good as my girlfriend, but it will do.

I needed to get a hobby after my girlfriend, Emma, stopped me sitting in the pub while she worked.

I was quite happy sitting there playing with my phone, supping beer and warning every guy off with a look when they tried it on with her. She keeps going on about me being jealous. It's not that. I trust her to the end. It's the local drunks and oddballs I don't trust, especially the new barman. He's a right wrong 'un. I know men, they'll jump on anything that they can, regardless of whether they have a boyfriend or not. I've listened to her, though. Well, it was that or not have a girlfriend. I can still go in on Fridays, she's agreed that, and she'll even throw free drinks into the deal. I can't moan at that. It does give me a fair amount of free time though, as she works every evening.

I'm out all day working on the roads, it's not bad money. Neither should it be; hanging about near motorways is not something I'd do for fun. People are nutters behind the wheel. I'm glad I'm no longer the new guy, they're the ones who have to put the first cone out when we're about to do some lane fixtures. I've been caught with more wing mirrors than I'd care to count. It's policy to report all 'incidents' (as the company calls them) to the police, although I've never heard of one driver in court for dangerous driving even though we've provided witnesses statements and license plates. It's just an almighty pain in the arse (and shoulder, usually) getting the paperwork together.

Anyway I digress. I needed a hobby and thought a nice modern one would do. We've recently had broadband laid in our village and I'd read that Xbox live was good. So I bought this. I love it. The only thing I don't like is getting beaten on Fifa by ten-year-old Japanese kids. They don't mind getting sworn at too much, either, they can't understand the words or they are laughing too hard to hear.

I've watched a couple of films on it, too. It's keeping me busy, that's for sure. The only time I'm not on it, in fact, is the hourly checks I make through the pub windows to make sure Emma is OK.

-Mark

RUMBA WOMAN SPANISH LADY FANCY DRESS COSTUME ONE SIZE

Fits my body in, no problem.

Brian asked me out the other night. Just marched up and did it. I thought he'd been chased by the way he almost ran in, but he explained he'd only just worked up the nerve to ask me out and needed to do it as he didn't want to lose the confidence. Said he'd been thinking about it for ages.

I've never been on a date before. I think my hump puts most men off and living in a village there is very little choice. Brian wasn't my first choice, admittedly. However as the old saying goes, 'Beggars can't be choosers'. It was nice to be asked. Being almost forty I'd started to worry that I'd never settle down and if that means I have to go with the man who messed himself on the ghost train and plays tennis on his own, then so be it.

This dress is nice, I thought I'd go a bit extravagant for the date, nothing's really 'fancy dress' unless you wear it to a certain kind of party, is it? And anyway, the open-necked style of the dress allows for my hump to breath. It gets spotty if I cover it too tightly. This was perfect. I'm glad I didn't listen to my mother and allow her to make me a dress or even worse her second suggestion, use her old wedding dress. She is always trying to re-use stuff. I'm so excited to find out where he is taking me.

-Janet

FANTASY VILLA — WOODCRAFT CONSTRUCTION KIT

Good enough to get you a girlfriend, but careful with the glue.

I decided I was giving up women. I had my first date the other night. It was going well. I asked all the questions of her, as suggested in a book I brought. I took her to a nice place, got a taxi — everything! Sixteen quid return that cost, plus tip. I paid for the whole meal, too. It nearly blew my whole fortnight's giro. I even rolled out my best joke about the penguin and his lunchbox and spent the evening complimenting her whilst looking at her face and not her chest (again read in my book) — mostly, anyway. I even let her choose the wine; well I'd had two bottles for confidence before I left my house. Finally, I'm absolutely certain I put on my best smile all night. I was the perfect date in every way. Did I get a good night frenzy in the back of the cab on the way home? No. It wasn't my fault Blind Barry was late collecting us, everyone gets lost once in a while.

I texted her the next day, asking if she'd got home OK and explaining again that I was sorry for vomiting on her a bit as I got out the taxi. I didn't get a reply. I spent ages checking my phone, walking into the garden to check the signal, switching it on and off, you name it I was doing it — nothing. No reply at all. I was gutted.

That's when I decided I needed something else in my life, a new hobby, something to take my mind off the crushing disappointment of a failed date. I've had a few hobbies in my time, none of which have been too successful. Sailing was a complete disaster, although I did get to ride in a lifeboat. The gardening was mildly successful, I ate one tomato before the others got blight.

Down to this woodcraft construction kit. I unpacked it immediately after putting on my hobby waistcoat, laid all the pieces in the hallway. First I checked to make sure they were all in the box, they were. I've actually written to a jigsaw maker and expressed my displeasure at finding a fifty-piece jigsaw was missing a bit. I'd got all the way down to the last bit and couldn't find it. It ruined the entire week. Once I'd counted all the bits of this kit I moved my project into the lounge. I didn't bother switching my phone off as Mum was at the bingo and no one else calls anyway, and I got to work. No offense to the makers, but if Janet had called I'd have happily binned this.

I'm not sure what happened after that, the last thing I remember is undoing the cap of the glue and taking a whiff to check if it was the proper stuff and not the rubbish white kind they give you in primary school.

The nurse who removed the little wooden roof tile from my face said I was lucky I'd been found or the glue would have finished me off. It seems I'd passed out face down on the glue so was breathing it in with every breath I took. Janet had come round and saw me through the window, then she kicked my back door in and tried her best to remove the glue tube that was hanging from my top lip. That had caused problems of its own, so she just put the cap back on, screwing my skin into the rivets as she went.

I seem to remember the ambulance being a very pretty colour but that was about it until I woke up in hospital with Janet at my bedside, which was a nice surprise.

Turns out I'd taken Janet's number down wrong and that I'd not got out the taxi half way home as I'd first thought. Janet had taken me in the house and got me as far as the sofa. I had been sick on her though, that was true.

We've decided to make this model together now and are

about halfway through. Janet takes the glue home with her, though, so I don't complete any without her.

I think we might be boyfriend and girlfriend now and it was this model that brought us together.

-Brian

MOLDEX 6400 — EARPLUGS — ROCKETS EAR PLUGS

Great if you live next door to an idiot.

I have the misfortune of living next door to an idiot. He isn't particularly malicious or evil. He's just an idiot. It's not a nice word but there isn't really a better one. If he's not creating havoc in the village and making people hate him even more than they already do, he is up to some hare-brained scheme in his house. Which unfortunately for me is attached to mine. Last week it was maracas, this week it was a triangle. To top off being an idiot, he is also tone bloody deaf. When he starts singing an' all I have to go out. It's like hearing a dog being put through a mincing machine before it's died. I've tried complaining to the council and they've been out, but they say they can't do anything as he's only doing what he likes in his own house, which is his right apparently — even if it completely ruins the ambiance of mine. I'm sure they'd only have to re-house him again anyway. In fact I suspect the only reason he has a three bed house is because he caused this type of problem in the flat he lived in before. It must have been even worse there, what with people surrounding him on all sides.

Drastic action was needed after a particularly bad summer. I've found him face down in his own garden after taking a kicking from some locals, I've seen him through the curtains face down at the table, groaning, I had to call his girlfriend that time — she took some convincing as she doesn't particularly like him either, I don't think.

I've decided I'm not helping him anymore, I've tried speaking to him about looking after himself and keeping his noise down but then he just tries to find music he thinks I'll like and play it louder, thinking that will solve the problem. Like I said, he's an idiot.

These plugs are the best thing since old Arthur died and he moved in. They don't fall out in the night, they don't get stuck and they keep the noise out. I don't hear anything when I wear them. The only issue is I can't hear my own TV when I have them in. Maybe the manufacturer could design something to help with this? Or a set of these that had little speakers in, that would really be something. I don't suppose I'll see such a wonder in my lifetime though. Sadly.

-Margaret Copperfield

REAL LIFE SIZE A XL SHEEP

So lifelike.

I managed to get myself in a terrible situation. I recently suffered a huge rejection in my personal love life. The woman I've loved for years flatly told me that she felt I loved alcohol and my parishioners more than I love anything else, including her. This is completely ridiculous as I am more than in control of my drinking. Fair enough, I sometimes go a little bit too far, but who doesn't? And as a vicar I have so much pressure on me to perform, it sometimes feels that the bottle is my only friend. After Mary Woodford had delivered her blow I turned to my old friend, Martel. I did particularly hit it a little harder than usual and at some point during that morning I must have decided to go for a drive and pick some more up or drive past Mary's house. I remember coming back down the hill towards the drive, I must have been really wasted as I hallucinated that a rocket was chasing me, I floored it to get away and that's the last thing I remember. When I woke up I'd completely missed my parking space on the drive and crashed through the paddock fence. Unfortunately one of the farmer's sheep was grazing just on the other side of the fence and was killed, hopefully instantly. Luckily for me, I live in the quiet end of the village so no one was around to see my little *faux pas*. The sheep was in a terrible state, there was no way he could have been saved. I'd managed to drag him a few hundred yards with the Volvo, too. It makes me emotional just to think about him. Almost in half, he was. I did the decent thing and buried him at sea. Well, river. I dragged the two parts of him down to the bank — he completely spilt on the way — and let him float his way to animal heaven. I couldn't bring myself tell the farmer, Bert, what I'd done.

To cover my trail I fixed the fence, best I could, raked the grass up where the tyres had made indentations and hoped he wouldn't notice one of his sheep gone while I went over to the next village to look for a replacement. It was a task and a half as the only sheep I could find in a ten mile radius belonged to Nasty George the well-known psychotic farmer in Corkville. I'm many things, but I'm not stupid and stealing one of nastys sheep would have been completely insane.

Scouring the internet for a solution I came across this little number. It was the only thing I could think of, so within 48 hours I had a replacement for Bert's sheep. All I had to do was go down to the lock, locate the top half of the original sheep and remove the identify tag and stick it on this. Then all I did was place the fake sheep across the paddock, under the apple tree.

Bert's been back from his trip for over a week now and the fake sheep is still in place, I've only moved it about in the dead of night twice and he still doesn't seem to have noticed.

5*: this thing really does look realistic.

-Father Frederick

PETE SORTWELL

20 X REUSEABLE WOODEN MOUSE RODENT TRAPS — QUICK ACTION

These look like they'd really hurt if they caught a human.

Some bugger killed my favourite sheep and dumped him in the river. Never harmed no one, Little Bertie didn't. I named him after myself and had already decided I'd be keeping him back from the slaughterhouse. Give him the run of the paddock and let the grandkids play with him.

I gets home from my holidays and find someone's either killed or stolen him. Not only that but they've replaced him with a life-sized fake sheep. I suspected it was Father Frederick from the vicarage next door. No proof, other than he is always drink-driving and I couldn't see his car, which is normally parked on the driveway.

I don't understand why he bothered to replace Bertie with a fake sheep. I've killed a couple of cows that weren't mine in the past, by mistake, of course. I either left them where they were or dragged them to the side of the road and denied all knowledge. This Muppet let himself down secondly as he kept creeping into the paddock late at night and moving the fake sheep about, thinking I wouldn't notice.

I decided to take action and bought 10 lots of these mousetraps, scattering them liberally over the paddock surrounding the fake sheep, and braced myself.

Two nights later I heard the Father's screams. I was right. The soppy old goat was rolling around in a big pile of traps and bloody squealing like a schoolgirl. He wasn't even making much effort to get up. Just rolling into more and more traps as he frolicked on the floor.

I didn't go and assist him. I just called the police who in turn called an ambulance and the Fire Brigade after the PCSO took one trap to the foot and refused to go any further. The brigade had to lay their ladder over the paddock and the ambulance men walked over that in order to reach the vicar.

I think he'd passed out by the time they reached him as the screaming had stopped. Good job too, because when he fell off the stretcher into another pile of traps he'd have really felt it had he been awake. I heard laughing coming from the crowd of emergency services and, looking over to see what had caused the merriment, I saw three well placed traps hanging right from the groin area of Father Frederick.

5*: these traps helped avenge the best sheep the world ever saw.

-Farmer Bert

THE BEST PUB JOKE BOOK EVER!: NO. 5 [PAPERBACK]

Top banter!

After a pretty harsh introduction to the locals on the night of my interview due to an unfortunate uniform choice, I decided I'd need to pull out all the stops to impress on my first night.

I got this book and started to learn the jokes in it, standing in front of the mirror practicing all the faces I thought the jokes would require and memorising the words. I've not been big on worded jokes before now, I'm more a practical joker. My favourite being putting laxatives into the food and drink of people I don't like. Most people find that funny. Well, all people except the person who consumes them. I thought I'd nailed down the deadpan look. The grinning smile was harder as I always think that if you laugh at your own joke then you're a bit of a tit — which I still stand by, however if I was to integrate into the local village community then I needed to make sure I was in the best position to do so and humour always works. I took the laxatives in case there was an uproar of laughter again, but hoped I wouldn't need to administer them.

The entrance went OK, there were a few elbows to people's ribs and nods over to me as I walked in but, once the purple jokes were done with it went well.

Two favourites are; 'Man goes into a library and asks for a book on suicide. Librarian says "F**K off! You'll never bring it back,"' and, 'Why did the pervert cross the road? Because he couldn't get his knob out the chicken.' However, my absolute best is one you play a little trick on the customer with. They come in, or, are sitting at the bar when I return and I say 'Cor, he's a dark horse, ain't he?' The customer always says 'Who? Who?' thinking they're about to get a bit of insider gossip. Then I simply say 'Black Beauty' and walk off. It gets them every time. I've even started something of a trend. We have a humpty dumpty version, 'He's in pieces,' and a Jack and Jill version, 'They're up and down'. No one has taken it the wrong way and this joke alone has done far much more for me than any purple outfit ever could have. If I knew where my mother was I'd get in contact and let her know.

I'm now fully living the village life. I've managed to get out of Jock's shed, and since learnt he'll do anything to get money off people. I'm grateful that I was able to stay in there for a bit, though, as if I hadn't I wouldn't be where I am now. I've got a room above the pub, free rent, and I'm close to getting into the manager's bedroom, if you know what I mean. *massive wink* All I've got to do is edge the competition out the way and I'm in.

On the whole it's not been such a bad summer. Except the shoeing I got while dressed as a Mexican.

-Terry

KODAK PLAYSPORT ZX5 FULL HD 1080P, WATERPROOF, DUSTPROOF AND SHOCKPROOF — AQUA

Handy and cheap! Just like the wife I'd like.

Unfortunately I managed to drop my old camera in the river trying to catch young Denny smoking drugs. I already had him on camera firing stones or something at Brian's CCTV and wanted to put the final nail in the coffin for him so his children's home would kick him out and he'd be moved away from us. It didn't work. So I blew the last of my bride funds on this new camera. It's not as good as the Panasonic V700, but it is almost there and cheaper. I've gotten quite into filming the local village residents. I was sitting by my bedroom window one day when I saw Father Frederick speeding through the village in his Volvo Estate. Now, we all know he drinks a little too much but this was the first time I'd seen him driving in such a manner, ever. Sitting at my bedroom window wondering what he was up to and watching the footage back I decided to wait as he'd have to return at some point. There is only one road down to his end of the village.

It only took about an hour for him to return and when he did I'd got bored at the window and decided to hide up the apple tree in the paddock opposite his house. I had a great view. I wanted to see if he fell out of the Volvo or just exited normally. I wasn't expecting to see what I did. Never in a million years. First I thought all my Christmases had come at once when Denny and his little mate came along looking shifty but sadly it wasn't the double scoop I thought it would be as they went off somewhere else. They must have got spooked. I'd have followed if I didn't think I'd capture something better.

Father Frederick drove into his drive faster than he'd gone past my house, crashed through a fence and then carried on towards me in the tree. I thought he'd seen me and was angry. Eventually the long grass slowed him down, although I think it was the sheep he hit and dragged along that really put the brakes on and he came to a stop just under where I was sitting. He'd passed out. The engine must have stalled when a bit of the sheep caught in it. This was incredible luck as if he'd have carried on he'd have smashed right into the tree I was perched in.

I checked his neck for a pulse like I've seen them do on 'The Bill' and shook him a little to try and rouse him, then shook him a bit more and then fully started slapping the absolute hell out of his face trying to wake him up. He murmured a bit, muttered some swear words about trying to sleep and nodded back off. This was enough for me so I got the full aftermath shot and walked back up the paddock following the tyre marks Father Frederick's Volvo had ploughed, although I dodged the bits of sheep that were lying about.

I'm in the process of setting up a new email address and seeing if I can blackmail him with the footage. After the 'You've Been Framed' misery, this seems like a good way to replace all the savings I've spent from my Thai bride fund. I should be able to get a full harem of brides for what this footage is worth!

5* for the camera, delivery was quick too, well done Amazon.

-David

ALCOHOLICS ANONYMOUS — BIG BOOK [HARDCOVER]

A nice present for an alcoholic.

An old friend of mine has recently, I hope, come to the end of his drinking in the most disastrous of ways. I've ordered him this book as a last chance saloon. Nothing else seemed to have worked. Me telling him I wouldn't be friends or anything more with him while he drinks doesn't seem to have done the trick over the last twenty years. I've tried, over the years, to manipulate him into seeking a solution but that, also, hasn't worked a jot. I'll take it to the hospital and see what results it gets.

-Mary

A nightmare for an alcoholic.

Having been in hospital for a few weeks now, and not having the use of my hands, I've had to have this read to me.

We're not there yet but Mary is getting closer to finally realising that I'm the only man for her. She comes in regularly and reads to me. She hinted the other day that once I'm sorted out we'll be together. I knew it would happen one day. I'll start letting Mary know I can use my hands in about a week or so. Once I know she is truly mine forever. She says I'll have to go to meetings when I'm out too. I'm not sure what they're like. I did see an episode of 'Cracker' once. It seemed to be a load of old men sitting about in a room crying about not being able to drink anymore. I don't fancy that much, I have to say. If it will keep Mary happy though I'll go to a few and see if I can teach them a thing or two about how to control their drinking like I can. The Lord doesn't like too much dishonesty, but then, I wouldn't be able to serve the Holy Communion If I didn't drink myself, would I? So it must be OK to drink in God's eyes. Once we're married I'll share my feelings on this with Mary, then she won't have the option of leaving me again.

It's not a bad book to listen to when you're laid up in hospital, but I'd have preferred a good Andy Mcnab.

Having said that, this could possibly be the book that gives me back what is rightfully, in the eyes of God, mine — Mary Woodford. That being the case it's 5 stars for a book that would otherwise have got 3.

-Father Frederick

Update: He seems really interested. I'm so pleased. Buy the book if you need to help someone.

-Mary Woodford

SEXY VALENTINE MESH LACE TRANSPARENT BABYDOLL CHEMISE NIGHTWEAR SLEEPWEAR NIGHT DRESS NIGHTDRESS + G-STRING ONE SIZE (FITS FOR UK SIZE 6-12)

If this doesn't work he's definitely a bender.

I'm bored with my current boyfriend. He's too jealous. It does my head in. It's the same old crap; 'It's not you I don't trust, it's the men' is his favourite line to justify near stalking me. I work in a pub and there isn't much in the way of other men, which makes his insecurity all the more frustrating. As if I'm going to run off with dirty Jock, simple Brian or old Father Fred, the vicar. It's ridiculous he would even think it.

Having said that, I've just hired a new potman, Terry. He used to work for the fair and after stopping here, decided to stick around. I need the excitement in my life so I've decided to finally allow my boyfriend the chance of being right (for once in his miserable life) and seduce Terry. We've had a couple of glances across the barrels in the cellar but I can't work out if he's scared of me as I'm his boss or he likes the sausage in the hotdog that is sexuality. I'm hoping he's more a bun kinda guy.

This chemise is perfect, I don't want to appear too slutty. But I want him to see what's on offer before he makes the move, rather than me being the one to have to ask. He's living on the third floor now so it won't be hard to catch him out.

I've, today, been and purposely broken his toilet up there so he'll have to come down. Once closing time comes all I'll have to do is wait for him to go up to his, have his dinner, then realise he needs to come down to my floor to use the bathroom here. To make sure he doesn't just wee in the bath or sink I've turned the mains off too. There is no way he cannot come down and when he does I'll accidently come out of my room wearing this beauty.

I can't wait.

-Emma

HOME BREW INGREDIENTS —
WOODFORDE'S WHERRY REAL ALE —
40 PINT HOMEBREW BEER KIT

Good but hard to hide.

Getting home from hospital to find your home cleared of alcohol is something no drinker should ever have to put up with. That's what happened to me, though. Mary, my new girlfriend, had cleared it out. She wanted me on a health kick, which meant no booze at all. I'd gone through the motions of wanting to pack it in when I was in hospital as Mary had wanted me to and agreed that she'd come back to me if I took life more seriously. I struggle with people telling me what to do, no matter how long I've loved them from afar. As soon as she left the first night (she won't stay over until we're married — it would set the gossips off) I searched all the places I used to keep drink. She'd cleared the lot. Even the bottles I kept on top of the wardrobe and the ones in the toilet cistern. I was parched, completely and utterly in need of a drink. Mary had also been to the pub and the shop telling them not to serve me, so I didn't even try. That would have made me look like I really had a problem. Begging for drink is never a good look. Although I would have done that if I thought they'd serve me. They wouldn't though; Mary was very persuasive when she wanted to be.

She'd even removed my wallet from the house, the credit card numbers from Tesco and Asda. The only place she hadn't got to was Amazon and this was all I could find. I needed to wait for the drink to brew but that was OK. I felt better just knowing it was on its way. It was kind of poetic that the first brew I started up was called Woodforde's as that's my girlfriend's last name.

It was dead easy to get the brew started, everything I needed was either in the box or in the shed. There's very little work to do once everything is in the pot brewing. That's pretty much it, stir it a couple of times and then it's a waiting game.

I think I lasted about half a day of drinking it before Mary busted my game. I shouldn't have been surprised, I was asleep in the garden during autumn, which is completely out of character for me. I don't sleep outside, least of all in the pouring rain and not in the daytime either. I woke up to thirty-one pints of ale being poured on me, and a terrible earache.

We've sorted it out now. The beer, as I remember it, was quiet pleasant, I'd have paid for it in a pub. While drinking it, though, I realised what everybody else had been saying to me for so long. I do like alcohol a little too much.

Mary has shown me the light. I've ordered, then thrown away, a couple more of these kits in the meantime during 'moments of madness' but I've not brewed since the first time. She'll definitely leave me if I do.

It's a nice kit, but I recommend people with a drinking problem don't bother with it.

-Father Frederick

Wentworth Large Chicken Coop Hen House Ark Poultry Run Nest Box Rabbit Hutch

Nice coop — be careful if you have evil chickens, though.

Being Valentine's day and being the romantic I am, I brought this coop for Janet. I thought she'd prefer it to a run of the mill normal, boring old engagement ring. I even built it for her in my back yard. She'll live with me once we're married anyway.

It wasn't easy to put together; the instructions didn't make sense. I can read and write pretty well, if I do say so myself, but the pictures-only diagrams had me completely stumped. It's a good job I ordered it in the January sales as by the time I'd got it done it was almost March. I was able to show Janet the almost finished product on the day and we were standing in the middle of it when I got down on one knee.

I've seen a lot of love films over the years. I'm keen on films, but love films are a favourite. You name it I've seen it. I was kind of expecting the proposal to go as I'd seen in the films; however, I now know that in this situation a ring is an essential item to be holding. Not, as I was, a roll of chicken wire. I admit it was stupid to think she would immediately say yes and help me put the wire on, which is undoubtedly a two man job, whichever way you try it. Janet got a little upset when I didn't laugh and pull out a ring after she asked if I was joking. Once I'd picked myself up after tripping on the ramp and pulling 75% of the last three months' work down, I chased after her and found her at her mothers', sobbing.

A week later when she'd calmed down, I'd got her a proper

ring and we'd agreed that chickens would not, in fact, be a symbol of our love, but a nice joint project instead. Janet agreed to be my wife and the mother to my chickens.

The coop is now finished. I have nine chickens in; they're named after the seven dwarfs, Snow White, and the Devil. I've called the black one the devil as I'm sure it has a deep-seated resentment of me. It goes wild with rage whenever I walk past and when I pop in to collect the eggs it attacks me with more gusto than a Pitbull. When I'm in the kitchen I can look out the window and his little beady eyes are on me, watching, waiting for me to come out so he can have another go. He is psychotically violent, If you could get chickens locked up for being mad, I'd definitely get the vet round to take him away. He is definitely the bird I'll be cooking for Christmas dinner.

The coop is fairly secure, I've only had to chase all the chickens back to it three times and two of those times it was my fault as I didn't latch it properly when trying to escape from The Devil.

The third time I'm not sure what happened. I came home from the town after being out all day and they were all out on the green, except the Devil, I couldn't see him anywhere. I managed to get them all back inside three hours — a new record. Once I'd sat in my chair, thanked God for taking The Devil away and started to relax I was set upon in the most horrendous manner — from behind! The Devil had somehow made his way into the house. He was going for my eyes, pecking me on the head and face, it really was a vicious attack. The police had to taser him as he was still going when they arrived. I'm not sure of the particulars I'd passed out long before.

It was a good job they did turn up as I think he'd started to eat the bits he was pulling off my face and clothes. I've recovered now, with the help of my loving fiancée. She's been so kind and loving. I've not yet found the courage to go out and feed the chickens yet but they haven't escaped again since that day. I'm not sure what happened to The Devil. Hopefully he's been destroyed by a hungry police dog.

In closing I don't think the coop was to blame for what happened, I think I'm unlucky and got given a bad chicken, I think the people knew he was evil as they put him in the box for nothing.

Janet and I will keep the chickens that are left, although I'm not sure if we'll get more.

I can't really fault the coop, they have loads of room and it did what I bought it for, it brought us closer to the dream of being man and wife.

-Brian

PERSUASION SKILLS BLACK BOOK: PRACTICAL NLP LANGUAGE PATTERNS FOR GETTING THE RESPONSE YOU WANT

Got me what I wanted.

My partner, for want of a better word, is a drunk. Always has been. I've always wanted to change that. To the point where I stayed away from him in the hope that he'd realise why I was doing it and stop. He didn't. For twenty years. So, I tried sitting and reading recovery books to him while he was in hospital following a drunken car crash. I've cleared his house of drink. I wasn't 100% confident that he wouldn't drink again, but I knew I wanted to be with him. That's when I came across this book. I wanted to plan what I'd do when he drank again.

After reading the section that applies to me I formulated my plan. I was going to have a tantrum. I'd not done it before. I was going to do that and do it really well.

It took about six weeks for the day to come when I needed to carry out my plan, however when that day came I put in a performance Dame Judy Dench would have been proud of. I ended up tipping a huge vat of beer he'd been brewing in the shed over him as he was rolling about on the ground, drunk.

The results seem to be good. He is now attending his AA meetings on a regular basis and has improved on many levels. He asks how my day was, isn't as selfish and is less angry when sober. In fact, he is like he used to be after two beers but before five — without the need to drink.

Now that I regularly use techniques offered in this book, I am getting quite good at getting what I want. All the tips about what words to use and what facial expressions to put on my face when using them have been absolutely fantastic. I'm turning into quite the master manipulator. I get better cuts of meat from the butcher, last week the neighbours finally cut the huge hedge they've been refusing to for years, every area of my life has got better as a result of reading this book.

I would highly recommend it for anyone who feels they have been walked all over for most of their life and wants a change.

-Mary

CHEERS — THE COMPLETE SEASONS BOX SET [DVD]

Cheers! (For bringing it out on DVD.)

While recuperating from a vicious chicken attack, I found myself a little bored and lonely. Lying around with my eyes covered by bandages is not my idea of fun. Janet was coming in when she wasn't at work, bringing me dinner and washing my face, but until I ordered her to get me this box set, I was pretty much just sitting in the dark silence of my living room waiting to get better.

Hearing Woody, Frasier and the gang did me the world of good. I could picture them sitting there in the bar as they spoke and went through the trials and tribulation of their daily lives. It helped my eyes work again as I know all the scenes and the facial expressions from watching my huge VHS collection over and over again. I'd not have bought this, but when the chicken attacked me in my own home I fell into the TV cabinet, landing on the video player. The TV made it out alive, but my beloved video player is now seeing out its days in the shed, a twisted pile of metal. Although I do have plans to make it work again one day.

I've eBayed the old video collection and hope to make at least thirty or forty pence.

This is a great TV show and I am so pleased that they've brought it out in a new format. The sound is crisper than the old version. Unfortunately I can't comment on the picture because at the time of watching, I couldn't see it. I bet it was good though.

I'll watch again in a couple of months, once I've finished with the Frasier box set I'm watching at the moment.

-Brian

SPARKLE HEARTS — PURPLE (METALLIC) CONFETTI MIX, 14G

A great disguise for hard rice.

I hate weddings and all the people that are involved in them. Everyone is so bloody happy. I've been married for years and it never made me happy or anything close. It made me miserable, having to cook, clean and look after a big baby. Men are like that, they never grow up and the more you do for them, unlike woman who appreciate it and return the favours, the more they want, no, expect, you to do for them. I don't buy confetti normally, I usually rip up newspaper that I've found in the street, but people seem to turn their noses up at that. On top of that they can always tell that is was me who put the hard rice in with the handfuls of paper. This stuff allows me to throw the confetti/rice mix into the groom's face and eyes with impunity.

This year I've had one wedding and it worked a dream. The handful of rice was well disguised between these love hearts. Because it's paper no one bats an eyelid at an older lady throwing with some effort, they all assume we have no power. I was able to get a good javelin-style launch of the handful I had that day. I was just reloading my palm when I noticed the groom wasn't where he'd been. Turned out I hit the jackpot first go and got a few bits past his mouth and straight down the back of his throat. He'd had to get on all fours and have his best man thump on his back. I couldn't believe my luck.

Unfortunately for me, though, the bride saw me celebrating

in the age old fashion of pretending I'm wielding an axe at alternate shoulders and dancing and pointed me out to the crowd.

I've now been banned from the church on wedding days. I'll think of something, though. It's my favourite hobby, I won't be kept from indulging for the sake of one lucky shot. In football players are celebrated for making the once in a lifetime shot of scoring from the other end of the pitch; in this sport I was ostracised from the churchyard.

Totally unfair.

-Ethel

JOY OF SEX: GOURMET GUIDE TO LOVEMAKING

Should come with a practice doll.

It's happened. I've finally gotten the green light. Janet and I have set the date that we're going to have sex! In less than two weeks' time, once the final chicken attack injuries are cleared up. I am literally busting at the seams with excitement. I've bought some fake flower petals, some girly music to play and I've scraped off the bed sheets. I'll probably have to do it again in the next two weeks, though, as I really am that excited.

I've looked through the book and I've made some notes. I've even practised a little bit with a couple of pillows that I gaffer-taped together — just the positions, nothing weird. They all seem fairly easy to get into, although I did feel a little pull in my back when I was testing out the thrusting. I test that bit a lot, actually. It did seem a little weird at first as I hadn't thought to attach any arms or legs to my fake Janet. I soon sorted that, though, with some large socks that I was saving for this year's Guy Fawkes and by putting a jumper on and tying the ends with string. I then had to undo it all and put some screwed up newspaper in so I could position the arms a little bit. I did the same with the socks. I didn't put a mask on as I only have a ghoul one left over from Halloween and that would have just been weird. I drew a face on the top pillow, though, then I changed the face to make it look like it was enjoying itself. I got that carried away in making my practise model that I almost forgot why I was doing it. Going at the pillow doll with some muster in my favourite position in the book I managed to achieve a level of confidence I was happy with. I made a bit of a mess of the pillows, what with the marker pen I'd used to draw the face on, the tape I'd used and the new stain I'd managed to make on it. The pillow case covered any indiscretion, though.

Over the last few days I've built and rebuilt the model a few times. It's like a hobby and learning at the same time.

I'll update in the comments section once I know if the practise has paid off.

-Brian

Update: It worked. I put in the performance of a lifetime. Janet was really impressed. Some of the positions seemed to not go down as well as others; Janet preferred to do the normal style. She was up for trying other things and seems to like going on top the best. I ended up buying some new sheets in the end, I'd have replaced the pillows and duvet if I'd have had some more money but, alas, the ruined old pillows needed to stay for a while. There was a little moment when after the third go the pillow cover came off a little and the face I'd drawn on exposed itself to Janet as she was reaching for it to lay down. She saw the funny side though and accepted that I'd drawn it on years ago. I won't be sharing with her my little hobby as, to be honest, that's still something I indulge in when Janet isn't here.

My only complaint it that it should come with a practice doll.

-Brian

PENIS ENLARGEMENT PUMP

Works — temporarily.

Turns out my love life isn't going to be the wild and passionate affair I'd read about in 'Fifty Shades of Grey'. My boyfriend, Brian, is pretty terrible. The outlook is not even good enough to be bleak. I had to go on top just to feel something rubbing on the hairs and the pants he was wearing were totally false advertising. It was more like a fig than a banana.

I bought this to try and help him get it just a little bigger, as I get more of thrill from brushing up against something on the bus. The problem is, he is really sensitive about the size of his chopper and it would devastate him if I was to present him this with a raised eyebrow and a wink. However, desperate measures call for desperate actions. I've been single since I was born and apart from a questionable affair with the vicar in my teens, I still count myself as a virgin — even after that boyfriend.

It's so small he didn't even realise it wasn't in. This is not something that can continue. So I thought long and hard about it, discussed it with my mother and between us we came up with a plan. Mother gave me some of her sleeping pills. She has loads that she's hoarded. I now put a few of them in his Robinson's squash before bed and once he's out for the count get this bad boy going. I'm not sure of the lasting results as yet but one thing is for sure. Once you start pumping with all the fury of a mid-thirties virgin it sure makes things bigger.

One night I wanted to really give it a good go, I was

pumping for at least an hour and a half and the penis was so swollen, I couldn't get it out the pump. I had to get my mother round to help. We both pulled and pulled but it was stuck fast. Mother even tried smearing some kind of grease she had in her shopping trolley around the end but that wouldn't shift. It was only after more frantic pulling that My boyfriend ejaculated and the pressure inside tube forced most of him out. Once he'd calmed down it was easy to remove the pump.

It seems as well as working whilst the pump is attached it is also enjoyable for the person involved.

It was a little strange having my mother there whilst this happened but she is cool. I'm not even sure if she knew what was happening.

I've since repeated the procedure and I'm fairly certain that this doesn't actually work very well. There has been a minor improvement, granted, but when it isn't on, the penis is too sore to do anything with and when it is on, all it seems to do is arouse him, which does make it a little bigger, maybe that is what 'enlarger' means?

I'll continue regardless, I need some sausage in my life.

-Janet

CLEARANCE SPEEDO MEN'S SWIMMING BRIEFS

Snug.

I bought these to wear on my honeymoon. It's hot in Turkey, apparently, so these are just what I'm after. It's the first holiday I've been on in thirty years. I've always had to stay in the village and take care of my flock.

Besides, summer is a busy time for the church, what with tea parties and garden shows and sales. It was sunny the other day here, so I tried on the swim wear, just to try it out. I put my dog collar on as well, though, just to make sure I was still respectable. Things have changed since the 70s. Back then it was good to be hairy, it's what we all aimed for. Apparently hair is to be mocked these days. I thought that it was women who needed to keep their 'area' trim and shipshape. Turns out it's something we all have to make sure of. I'm not sure I will, though. I'm pretty old school on men's grooming. If it grows it stays, that's my motto, along with only combing what's on my head. Anything else and the church would have me out for being a bit 'funny'. Just like they did with Perfume Derek.

Mary turned out to the party just as I was being bundled into Mrs White's conservatory by her burly sons, wrapped in a blanket. She thought I'd gone back on the drink. I explained at great length that I was just testing out my new holiday swimming trunks and in the end, after a little bit of pleading and an enforced breath test, she believed me. Not before the White brothers had taken my breath test as a form of attack and dragged me off her, though. It was all sorted out in the end and Barry, one of the sons with a particularly interesting name, lent me one of his gym tracksuits to get home in without causing any more offence.

On a comfort note, the Speedos ARE snug, yes. That's a given, however they keep everything naughty where it should be. I'm not so blessed in the groinal zone so there is no need to worry about outline or the odd testie hanging out in the breeze without noticing. As with all Speedos they have the non-see-through fabric sewn in, so there is no issue there either.

If it wasn't for the prudes in the village I live in I would have had the perfect trunk experience.

I can't wait to get to a hotter climate where hair doesn't matter and people wearing just pants are normal.

-Father Frederick

YORK CAST IRON KIT IN A CASE — 20KG

Just right for someone just out of prison.

I got into weights while staying at the Young Offenders' Institute. I wasn't there long enough to get big, though.

I also wasn't there long enough to avoid having to go back to the children's home either. It's a bit better there, though, as most of the staff have changed. The other kids say there was a massive investigation after I was in court. The new guys don't take any nonsense. I'm on curfew and to be honest don't feel like breaking it. These weights come in handy for when I'm at home. I've been off the weed since the day I got out, too, I didn't even go and check my crop at Father Frederick's. I'll leave that. No doubt he's found it by now anyway.

I don't really want to see the old fart anyway. It's his fault I got caught. If he hadn't brought the bud I'd left under his kitchen table to the home I would never have been caught and the stuff I had under my mattress wouldn't have been found. The dozy old swine didn't have a clue what he was doing, he thought it was for cooking with!

It was an agency worker who called the police. The social worker had come on shift by the time the search finished and hadn't looked happy. He was my case worker and we didn't get on. Just to get him back for being an ass I pointed the finger at him as I was being led out. 'He knew about it all,' I shouted. Then for authenticity I added that I knew he had some more of the stuff in his car. Turns out he did have something in his car he didn't want the police to see and his beetroot face instantly told them that. I wasn't around to see what it was and the other kids were all kept in the lounge, but he never returned. Good. He was rubbish anyway.

My new worker, Gary, wrote me a plan to do these weights. We also speak about family stuff. He talks to me about my mother in a nice way, not like the old one used to.

These weights could be the start of something new. Gary says if I behave and get all my school work done then he'll take me to the boxing gym, I can't wait for that.

If you're looking for something to be able to change your life around these are a good starting point.

-Denny

HIS & HERS 8MM/6MM TUNGSTEN CARBIDE CLASSIC WEDDING BAND RING SET (AVAILABLE SIZES H — Z+2) EMAIL US WITH YOUR SIZES

Perfect. Cheap and don't look it. Just what I like.

Being on Benefits usually means that you have to go without. These rings cost me £59 for both. Janet and I married three weeks ago. The Community Care grant and some of the money Janet's Nan left her made sure we had enough to have the day we wanted and deserved.

Janet looked beautiful. I cried like a baby — not at the amount of people who didn't turn up to the church, but at the feeling of someone loving me enough to walk down the aisle of a pretty much empty church. I was glad the cleaners stopped working and took a seat for a while, it made it feel like it wasn't totally empty. Janet had a couple of friends and family there, her mum and dad and my mum, along with Mary Woodford, completed the guest list. I invited the whole village via a poster in the pub, but it must have fallen down as no one came. Father Fred seemed to be sober for once, too, I think that's got something to do with Mary Woodford. They are an item now and we joked before the service that it would be their wedding next time. We had a traditional ceremony, no rubbish. The organ had broken, which was OK as we didn't have a player anyway. Father Frederick had some songs on cassette and we sang along to them, that worked well. The tape only creased at one point and what with Father Frederick being the only one who wasn't miming we hardly noticed. The rings were a great fit, if a bit snug on me. Janet says I have sausage fingers and was worried she wouldn't be able to find a ring to fit me. This did without any issue though.

Janet says getting a little bit of confetti in the eye is good luck, so I shouldn't worry about it. It did smart a bit, but it wasn't as bad as the bit of rice that went down my throat. I had to cough it up. I wasn't going to let a bit of dry rice ruin the day, though, so once I'd finished retching I got up and we continued with the day. Turns out it was Janet's mum chucking rice. It must have got mixed up somehow. She seemed really happy Janet was getting married. Seeing Ethel dancing about with joy outside the church was nice to see.

We held the meal and drinks party at the Lamb and Whistle. Cold cuts, salad and more sparkling wine than we could drink. Most people in the village had been working, they said, which was why they couldn't make it to the church. I was pleased they turned up in the end, though. Even if I do suspect it might have had something to do with the free drinks. Well, that's what Janet said. I'm just happy the dog dirt attacks have stopped. Next year I'll be able to walk around the fair with no fear of being lynched.

It's been a great year on the whole.

-Brian

MR AND MRS DUCK GIFT BOX SET

Who doesn't like wedding ducks?

Somehow that fool, Frederick, has managed to sort himself out. Earlier this year I'd thought I was going to have to release him from his role. However he's amazed me and re-ignited my faith in God above. Above all, he has managed to stop drinking. He's also, unbelievably, managed to get the woman I had in my office crying many, many times over his stalking of her, to marry him. I couldn't be happier. Not only is one of my wayward vicars a reborn man, I have got one of the major PR problems of the church out my office.

I bought them these ducks to celebrate. Everyone likes ducks, don't they? I do anyway.

I'm looking forward to doing the service.

Fingers crossed Ethel manages to aim her rice well that day!

Praise Jesus!

-Bishop Desmond

PETE SORTWELL

ABOUT THE AUTHOR

Pete is 33 and lives with his wife, Lucie; daughter, Lilly; and their pet sofa, Jeff. He's been writing for just under three years and they've been pretty eventful; well, more eventful than he thought sitting on Jeff, typing, would be, anyway.

First published in the *Radgepacket* anthology with a story he'd written during month five of his new hobby, Pete's now featured in a total of ten different anthologies and has been amongst some very fine company. (Although he was the best in all of them, he knows that because both his mum and Jeff told him and they're both honest-to-God Christians ... possibly.)

Author of comedy e-books *The Village Idiot Reviews*, *The Office Idiot Reviews*, *The Idiot Government Reviews* and *More Village Idiot Reviews*, Pete has seen these books sell more than he ever thought they would, and he's hooked. *Dating in the Dark* is Pete's first self-published novel. His traditionally published novel, *So Low, So High*, was published by Caffeine Nights in June 2013.

Contact Pete:

Facebook:
https://www.facebook.com/pages/Pete-Sortwell/255907757862913

Twitter: @petesortwell

email: petesortwell@googlemail.com

OTHER TITLES

SO LOW, SO HIGH

Most people generally don't drink white cider for breakfast, don't use the aisle of Tesco as a toilet and don't steal from their family and friends. Simon Brewster does though. He's a doomed man. Living life day to day, stealing Edam balls and legs of lamb, ducking and diving his way from petty theft to dealer and back again. If he doesn't change his ways, he'll never see middle age, let alone old age.

He's seen his parents on their knees, crying, begging him to stop; he's been arrested by his former best mate; he's been hospitalised, all as a result of drugs and alcohol. It's just not enough to make him stop.

Simon lies to everyone, including himself. The truth is, he has no more idea why he does the things he does than you do. What he needs is a way out. But if such a thing exists, Simon hasn't had much luck finding it. He's powerless and his life is unmanageable to the point of insanity.

This is the story of Simon Brewster's last year using class A drugs. Join him as he crashes his way through police cells, courtrooms and display cabinets. One way or another, Simon will stop using drugs. But can the people that love him help him overcome his addictions before his addictions destroy him?

Available from Caffeine Nights Publishing.

THE OFFICE IDIOT REVIEWS

There are all sorts of idiots we have to work with every day. Every office has them. Fortunately for most of us idiots in the work place are few and far between. However, Hogsbottom Plugs, 'the home of bath plugs' has a higher concentration than other workplaces, from the MD down to the cleaner, they're all Idiots.

Read the trials and tribulations of this idiotic workforce as they explain their recent life events through reviews of things they've bought. There's Donald, who try as hard as he does, simply cannot get the office junior to notice him, let alone drink some of his special, sleeping tablet-laced tea. Learn how Jeff gets his own back on the people who mock him by re-enacting a video he saw on YouTube involving seagulls, and watch in horror as the over-worked cleaner tries to solve the mystery of who is making his job of cleaning the toilets worse than a job cleaning toilets is already.

If you've ever worked in an office, then this is the book for you. You'll recognise the office sex pest, the liar and the moaning admin worker who's been there longer than the chairs. Written in the form of product reviews, *The Office Idiot Reviews* is the second in the series of 'Idiot Review' books from Pete Sortwell.

THE IDIOT GOVERNMENT REVIEWS

We've all seen the news over the last few years, watching in wonder and disbelief at the situations the people entrusted to run the country get themselves into and then proceed to lie their way out of. Just imagine, and this won't be hard, that they were so stupid that they wrote reviews of the items that got them into or out of their latest bit of trouble and posted them online.

Ted Williebond is angry, not only at having to settle for running the opposition, but also for the bullying he had to endure at school by Cameron Davies and Gary Osburn, who now run the Government and don't mind pointing that out to Ted every time they see him. Join Ted as he foolishly leaves reviews of such items as Silly String, vodka and thick curtains as he tries his hardest to bring down the coalition.

On the other side of the fence we've got Daniel Dangly, a foolhardy old school politician from Southamptonshire who, try as he might, cannot outrun the press, who seem to stalk him for easy stories; and Elouise Munch, a career girl more concerned about who's defaced her designer handbag than the people in her constituency.

Running the show though isn't Cameron Davies or Ted Williebond; in fact it is Betty Rivers, the CEO of Information Inc.

It can't work out well, can it?

Welcome to *The Idiot Government Reviews*.

THE COMPLETE IDIOT REVIEWS

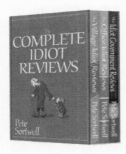

The first three 'Idiot' reviews books are now available from Amazon in e-book format as a handy box set.

MORE VILLAGE IDIOT REVIEWS

It's been a year since their last outing. Brian, Ethel and Father Frederick are back with more village idiocy.

Frederick has injured his nipples in a vicious moped accident whilst on his honeymoon and no longer feels like a man. He's taken up the drink again and is making people's lives a misery with his antics again. He can't work out why strange men keep following him while he's out drink-driving, though.

Brian's concentrating on getting through married life while trying to find a hobby that doesn't hurt. His cousin Jeff (from *The Office Idiot Reviews*) has moved in for the summer and is on hand to help Brian with his assertiveness when he is bullied by the local biker, Jock.

Ethel has discovered that it was Denny who made her shopping trolley explode last year and with Denny now an adult and living outside the safety of the children's home, it won't be long before she exacts the revenge she's been after.

Meanwhile a battle for power is taking place at the manor house. Lord Monty, who ordered his title from the Internet, is in a battle of wills with his gamekeeper, Chopper. It's a never ending struggle which, time after time, leaves Monty either out of pocket, in pain or soaking wet.

Written entirely in the form of product reviews, we guarantee you've never read a book quite like this before. (Unless you read the first one.) Hilarious and wholly original, *More Village Idiot Reviews* introduces the most bonkers set of countryside dwellers you've ever had the pleasure of meeting.

DATING IN THE DARK
Sometimes Love Just Pretends To Be Blind

Jason is single and has been for all of his 32 years. It's depressing. But not as depressing as being told by his mother that he looks like Humpty Dumpty — after the accident. With a face that not even his own mother can love, it's hardly surprising that he'll try anything to get a woman to go out with him, even if it's only for a single date. With little interest in anything other than his quest for a woman and a nice bit of cod and chips, Jason needs to think outside the box if he's going to find someone who'll give him a chance. Along with Barry — his best mate — Jason comes up with the only thing he thinks will work: dating a blind woman. However, to do that, he needs to pretend he's blind himself, which is a lot harder than you might think ... especially when guide dogs are so hard to come by. Eventually Jason's efforts pay off and he meets Emma, a pretty professional with a host of friends. When he takes her out, they instantly hit it off. But will Jason be able to fool both Emma and her best friend Jerry into thinking he's blind? With everything to play for, Jason faces the biggest challenge of his life, and nobody — especially not him — can see how it'll all turn out.

BRIDE AND GLOOM
Sometimes Love Is Better Off blind

In the first book of the 'Sometimes love ...' series, 'Dating in the Dark: sometimes love just pretends to be blind', Jason Harding thought he'd committed the ultimate betrayal. No, not cheating; he pretended to be, you guessed it, blind. For Emma, the woman he was stupid enough to think he was fooling, it wasn't anything like a betrayal. It was both sweet and sad at the same time and, as people in relationships have a tendency to do (if they don't split up because of one party's wild lies), Emma and Jason decide to get married.

Just how Jason manages to deal with the huge life change that is marriage is what this book is about. From getting his specially made suit tailored to his short height, to trying to keep a lid on his best man's plans for a wild weekend in Liverpool, he is going to struggle to make to through to the wedding without having a full nervous breakdown. His second best friend, Boris, also returns in this book, although he has lost his taxi, his wife and his ability to seem sober even when he's drunk six litres of vodka.

Jason is foolish enough to add Neil, Emma's wayward cousin, and Terry, the owner of Jason's favourite fish and chip shop, to his list of groomsmen. This is the fairly tragic band of men that are to ensure Jason makes it to the church on time, in possession of both his of his eyebrows and, of course, the rings ...

THE DIARY OF AN EXPECTANT FATHER

Not only is Graham Peterson unlucky in his choice of careers, he's also been terrible with women throughout his adult life. That changes when he meets Alison on a work night out. Unfortunately for Graham, however, things change so drastically that within a month of dating Alison he gets the news that he's about to become a father for the first time.

The Diary of an Expectant Father charts the months leading up to what should be the happiest day of a young couple's life, but with a relationship so new and a career so bad, can Graham keep everything together for the sake of his unborn child?

With all the pitfalls and worries of an expectant father charted, this book is for all those who have been through pregnancy or just want to know how a man deals with all these things internally.

THE DIARY OF A HAPLESS FATHER

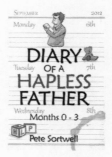

Not only is Graham Peterson unlucky in his choice of careers, he's also been terrible with women throughout his adult life. That changed when he met Alison, but within a month of meeting, he got the news that he was about to become a father for the first time.

The Diary of a Hapless Father charts those first three terrifying months of parenthood. With all the angst and fear of a new father, Graham needs to pull his socks up if he's going to become the father he always dreamed he would be.

With all the pitfalls and worries of a new father charted, this book is for all those who have been through early parenthood or just want to know how a man deals with all those things internally.

6328486R00088

Printed in Great Britain
by Amazon.co.uk, Ltd.,
Marston Gate.